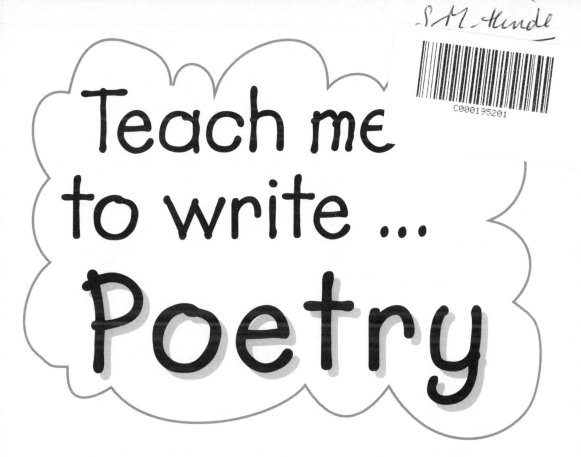

Teach me to write ... Poetry

A GUIDE FOR TEACHERS

Alan Gibbons

Nash Pollock
Publishing

© Alan Gibbons

First published 2005
Published by
Nash Pollock Publishing
32 Warwick Street
Oxford OX4 1SX

10 9 8 7 6 5 4 3 2 1

Orders to:
York Publishing Services
64 Hallfield Road
Layerthorpe
York YO31 7ZQ

A catalogue record of this book is available from the British Library.

ISBN: 1 898255 46 6

Design and typesetting by Black Dog Design, Buckingham
Printed in Great Britain by Hobbs the Printers

Contents

Acknowledgements

Many thanks to Carol Canavan, Catherine Carson, Linda Richardson, Phil Newton, Anne Gray, Steve Jorgensen, Bryan Wynne, everyone at Flintshire and Denbighshire LEAs, Angela Bradshaw and the Surrey English team, Maureen Pavey, Knowsley LEA, and all the youngsters I have worked with.

The author and publishers are grateful to the following for permission to publish copyright material: Five Leaves Publications for 'I Was Naughty Once' by Nicola Trew, from *Did I Hear You Write* by Michael Rosen; Gareth Owen for 'Conversation Piece' and 'My Granny is a Sumo Wrestler'; the estate of Adrian Henri and Rogers, Coleridge and White Ltd for 'Tonight at Noon' by Adrian Henri; Paul Cookson for 'Let No-one Steal Your Dreams' and 'It's Not the Same Anymore'; Jackie Kay and Bloomsbury Publishing for 'No Word of a Lie' from *The Frog Who Dreamed She was an Opera Singer* by Jackie Kay; Celia Warren for 'Football Training'; Trevor Millum and Resource Education for 'Song of the Homeworkers', from *Warning: Too Much Schooling Can Damage Your Health* by Trevor Millum; Faber and Faber for 'Roman Wall Blues' by W H Auden. 'I Know Someone Who Can' from *Quick, Let's Get Out of Here* by Michael Rosen (© Michael Rosen 1983) is reproduced by permission of PFD (www.pfd.co.uk) on behalf of Michael Rosen. 'Bradford' by Roger McGough from *Gig* (© Roger McGough 1973) is reproduced by permission of PFD (www.pfd.co.uk) on behalf of Roger McGough. The publishers would be pleased to hear from any other copyright holders whose copyright they may have inadvertently infringed.

My thanks to all the young poets whose work is included in this book.

Dedication

To Pat Horobin, a dear friend and memorable teacher

Chapter 1

Poetry in the Classroom

The insidious mastery of song

The first thing to confess, is this: I'm not a poet. There, I've said it. The first book in this series was about children writing fiction. This could be considered my main area of expertise. For fourteen years I have been writing novels, picture books and short stories for young people. In that period I have only a handful of published poems to my name. So why write a book about children writing poetry? Simple really: I love working with young writers and I love poetry. Helping youngsters produce poetry that reflects their ability to use and enjoy language has been one of my greatest pleasures as a classroom teacher, and it all stems from my own love of reading as a child. The first poem I remember that really swept me away was this one:

Piano

D. H. Lawrence

Softly, in the dusk, a woman is singing to me;
Taking me back down the vista of years, till I see
A child sitting under the piano, in the boom of the tingling strings
And pressing the small, poised feet of a mother who smiles as she sings.

In spite of myself, the insidious mastery of song
Betrays me back, till the heart of me weeps to belong
To the old Sunday evenings at home, with winter outside
And hymns in the cosy parlour, the tinkling piano our guide.

So now it is vain for the singer to burst into clamour
With the great black piano appassionato. The glamour
Of childish days is upon me, my manhood is cast
Down in the flood of remembrance, I weep like a child for the past.

The poem is contained in one of my old schoolbooks entitled *Selected Poems of the 20th Century*. It introduced me to Edwin Muir, W. B. Yeats, Ted Hughes, Robert Frost and many more. It is a wonderful collection and I still use it when I am working with teachers and young people. It must have been issued to me in the mid-nineteen sixties at Crewe Boys' Grammar School. It is bound in brown paper (of course!) and some time in my teens I pasted a Tolkienesque picture in the inside cover. I don't quite know why I still have the book. Was I awarded it for some long-forgotten achievement? I don't think so. Our education back then was rigorous rather than encouraging. Did I purloin it in a wicked moment? I sincerely hope not. More likely, it sat neglected and forgotten on one of my bookshelves through the dark storms of my adolescence until I rediscovered it some time after leaving school.

Why did Lawrence's poem affect me so deeply? To begin with it evoked the poet's relationship with his mother, his childhood, his home with astonishing power in its few spare lines. Reading those lines I felt the thrill of recognition. Then there was the language. Phrase after phrase I memorised:

'... the boom of the tingling strings ...'
'... The glamour of childish days is upon me ...'
'... the great black piano appassionato ...'
'... my manhood is cast down in the flood of remembrance ...'

The whole texture of the writing seemed so astonishingly rich. But one line stood out above all the others. It was this one, of course:

'... the insidious mastery of song'

That seemed to say it all. Many times since I have been made aware of that insidious mastery, either by songs themselves or by the sheer musicality of poetry. 'Piano' is one of the pieces of writing that made me an eager reader all my life. If there is one word that explains that attachment to reading it is *appassionato*. Now some in education take the line that the teacher has to explain everything. Leave any recess in the young learner's mind untouched by your searching pedagogy and you have failed. Any word you don't know, any concept you haven't grasped, get out that dictionary, thumb through that text book. I don't agree with that approach. Sometimes the reaching for meaning is a more important experience than the having of it. Rather than being handed an apple from the tree of knowledge it might be better to plant a stray seed and see what grows. Learning is an active process of exploration, not the passive receipt of gobbets of knowledge by waiting empty vessels.

So I never did look up the word appassionato. I was happy simply to reach for it. It was mysterious, and mystery buzzes with creativity. I had an inkling what it meant because the word *passion* was hidden within it and it sounded like a musical term. I still wasn't entirely sure of the full meaning, however. Did it matter? Did it detract from my enjoyment? Not one iota.

Now, what did I get out of reading 'Piano'? Did it improve my understanding of sentence structure, syntax and grammar? Possibly, but only indirectly. There was no instruction. Did it make me a better speller? I doubt it, though I could now spell appassionato. Mind you, I don't think I have ever had the opportunity to use the word until now. Did I garner new comprehension skills?

Well, not in the sense of answering 'correctly', no. But did it enrich my life? Absolutely! Many times during my near twenty year teaching career I despaired of the regular pressures placed upon us teachers to make English as a subject utilitarian and skills-based. Yes, children need the basic tools to express themselves orally and in reading and writing. But they want to express *themselves*. If the English curriculum is made entirely and exclusively subservient to the needs of the job market a huge amount is lost.

What do you remember about your school days? Is it the spelling test? Is it the exam revision period? I hope not. No, it has to be the odd *Wow!* moment you experienced: the time you starred in that production of *Othello*; the time you had to read your poem to the whole class; a special school trip; a teacher who found an anecdote to prise open new precincts of being within you. The fewer the *Wow!* moments the more impoverished the experience of education becomes. The question I wish to pose is this: why does the young child want to read and write? Surely it is because it is enjoyable and meaningful to them, not because 'One day it will get you a good job', or even worse, 'Because it is part of your national heritage.' Those basic skills we hear so much about are best practised in the context of an activity which is purposeful, engaging and enjoyable.

That is why, as a teacher, no matter which way the prevailing pedagogical wind was blowing, no matter what the latest ring-bind folder said, I always started by looking at poems themselves, not at what they were for or what the third word on line seven meant. For the first ten minutes every morning in my classroom we listened to music, sometimes discussing whether the sounds represented anything, sometimes just listening. Other times I would tell the youngsters about the composer's life or the times in which he or she lived. I might reminisce about its impact in a particular film. If we were listening to a song we might try to get a handle on the lyrics. I might even tell them what a song like 'Waterloo Sunset' meant to me.

In other words, I shared. I shared my reading, my memories, my hopes, my dreams. I shared myself. And that is an important point. Goodness help us if teachers are reduced to the status of impersonal teaching machines, beavering away to the insistent rhythms of attainment targets and programmes of study, objectives and strands. What makes a teacher special is the ability to connect. Teaching is a human construct, not a bureaucratic one. Anyway, not only did we immerse ourselves in music, but immediately before lunchtime and home time we always had a session sharing stories and poems. We didn't analyse them. We didn't deconstruct them. Whisper it, reader, we enjoyed them! Soon the youngsters would be calling out for their favourites: 'Can we have "Mr Moore" Again?' 'Do "Slow Reader".' 'No, make it "Goodbat Nightman".'

It was only on the basis of that enjoyment that I would ever be presumptuous enough to try to teach the children how to write poetry. There had to be exuberance, fun, entertainment. I just don't see the point of saying: 'Here is a poem you're probably not going to like, but it is a classic so open wide and take the medicine. A lot of clever people say poetry is good for you. Now let's see how we can write our own versions. I'm going to show you alliteration and versification, things you will need to understand in order to pass your tests.'

If I, somebody who always read for pleasure and was in the A stream of a 1960s grammar school, hated that approach at school, what hope is there for the child who hasn't had access to books and isn't the keenest academically? It isn't the function of poetry that we need to communicate to the kids, it is the value of it to them personally: the sheer fun, thrill and joy of it. Only within that context can teachers hope to teach them anything about language and its possibilities.

Memorable speech

OK, are you with me so far? You should be. After all, I've quoted D. H. Lawrence, a *name*. He writes poetry, no doubt about it. He's on the syllabus, part of the literary canon. But while I do use Lawrence, Sylvia Plath, Edwin Muir, Ted Hughes and Elizabeth Jennings in my writing workshops, I also use Ian McMillan, Benjamin Zephaniah, Michael Rosen, Paul Cookson, Adrian Henri, Brian Patten, John Agard, Lemn Sissay and Levi Tafari. Literature, if it is to mean anything to children, has to speak to them. It is a living thing. It breathes, it grows, it develops. The overwhelming majority of modern poets are aware of the literary tradition, the canon. They build upon it but they also subvert it. They use it as one possible starting point but they also use speech, popular music, rhyme and chant from many cultures. They may stand on the shoulders of giants but they do not have to remain in the shadow of those giants. People who become preoccupied with whether a piece of writing is literary or not forget that, to be creative, writing must change. The moment it starts repeating itself, it becomes ossified.

This is Mike Rosen writing: '... my work is a rag-bag of styles and genres, according to orthodox literary criticism, but does it matter? I'm not trying to hoodwink anyone, I'm not trying to gain membership to a Peerage of Poets. I write "bits" and "stuff".' (from *Did I Hear You Write?*)

So what is poetry? Michael Rosen quotes W. H. Auden and John Garrett's introduction to the 1935 anthology *The Poet's Tongue*. I have tried hard to find a better definition but I have had to slink back, tail between my legs, to one which has already been quoted extensively elsewhere. Well, what the heck? The reason it is quoted so widely is because it is good!

'Of the many definitions of poetry, the simplest is still the best: "memorable speech." ...

... All speech has rhythm, which is the result of the combination of the alternating periods of effort and rest necessary to all living things and the laying of emphasis on what we consider important ...

... poetry can appeal to every level of consciousness ...

... One must not let people think either that poetry never enjoys itself, or that it ignores the grimmer aspects of existence.'

That, to be honest, is my starting point in teaching poetry. From Homer to Basho (inventor of the Haiku), from Shelley to Brecht, from Hans Magnus Enzensberger to Simon Armitage, it's all stuff, it's all memorable speech. It is produced in a myriad of forms and it can all be enlisted to draw children into the Wonderful World of the Word.

Moving on with my tale, I've described how D. H. Lawrence's 'Piano' helped get me reading. It drew me into the insidious mastery of song. It was another poem which made me want to be a writer. Here it is:

Futility
Wilfred Owen

> Move him into the sun –
> Gently its touch awoke him once,
> At home, whispering of fields unsown,
> Always it woke him, even in France,
> Until this morning and this snow.
> If anything might rouse him now
> The kind old sun will know.
>
> Think how it wakes the seeds, –
> Woke, once, the clays of a cold star.
> Are limbs, so dear-achieved, are sides,
> Full-nerved – still warm – too hard to stir?
> Was it for this that clay grew tall?
> – O what made fatuous sunbeams toil
> To break earth's sleep at all?

Now this was writing. It was elemental, primal in its impact on me. The emotional effect was electrifying. Once more the language was musical and magnificently affecting. What probably impressed me most in Owen's poem was his ability to craft a beautiful sentence. How many times was I bored witless in English language lessons by précis and comprehensions, by clauses, main and subordinate? But here was Wilfred Owen achieving modulated, carefully crafted and supremely evocative sentences to insert a sliver of ice into the ventricles of my heart. I think I must have stared dumbly at these impenetrable sentences. Overawed, I knew I would never fashion anything so beautiful. What's more, no matter how much comprehension work we did in class, I didn't have a clue how Owen did it. The poem's face was as inscrutable as that of any ancient oracle. It seemed like magic, still does to be honest.

Thinking back on this experience in adult life, however, I knew that, to be a writer and a teacher, I had to break the code somehow, find a way to craft units of meaning which, though never reaching the heights Owen achieved, might provoke a response in the reader. Getting children to produce 'their own' versions of well-known poems seems pretty sterile. What teachers can do, however, is to use a loved poem (and it must be loved before it becomes the subject of 'modelling') to understand how certain structures work, how to achieve certain effects.

This can have two reasonably desirable outcomes:
• It can help deepen the child's appreciation of the poem. Sure, they may never write poetry themselves when they grow up, but if, by playing with the language of a poem they have enjoyed, they build a relationship with it, they will have gained something from the experience.
• They will, by interacting with many different pieces of writing, develop a repertoire of skills, models and templates. Over time they may synthesise these into something original of their own, or use them to focus ideas they already have, waiting to be turned into marks on the page. Most children find it difficult to 'just create' so it helps to draw on good quality models when you are trying to develop your own voice. As you mature you can take from them what you will, but having them in your tool box, the intellectual reservoir of skills, models and forms you construct, is important.

There is one more poem I would like to share with you. This is the poem that made me want to teach children how to write:

Roman Wall Blues
W. H. Auden

> Over the heather the wet wind blows,
> I've lice in my tunic and a cold in my nose.
>
> The rain comes pattering out of the sky,
> I'm a Wall soldier, I don't know why.

The mist creeps over the hard grey stone,
My girl's in Tungria, I sleep alone.

Aulus goes hanging around her place,
I don't like his manners, I don't like his face.

Piso's a Christian, he worships a fish;
There'd be no kissing if he had his wish.

She gave me a ring but I diced it away;
I want my girl and I want my pay.

When I'm a veteran with only one eye
I shall do nothing but look at the sky.

One time, in the late nineteen eighties, I was wondering how to teach the Romans to a Year Three class. Wasn't there a poem I read back about the time the Beatles were buying a ticket to ride? I dug it out and Eureka! I realised I would never need a worksheet again (well, I might steal that outline drawing of a centurion!). Auden's poem is witty and perceptive. It has a great rhythm. It is fun to perform and to listen to, and it teaches more about what it was like to be a Roman on Hadrian's Wall than an entire project loan of non-fiction books. I realised that, with a little bit of thought, many of those things which seem so laborious to teach can be communicated in the process of re-creating a poem the children have enjoyed. After this shaft of light on the way to Damascus – well, Prescot actually – we wrote:

- elegies for fallen warriors
- obituaries for Julius Caesar
- letters home from Gaul
- a Roman soldier's graffiti in the barracks
- diaries of a campaign against the Germanic tribes
- advertisements for gladiatorial combats
- a Boudicca war chant
- a Roman soldier's marching song.

These and many more were penned in the course of a term on the Romans and almost all in the form of poetry.

In this way I, as a teacher, was able to accumulate a series of poetic forms and use them across the curriculum. Worksheets and note-taking might communicate information but they didn't bring history (or, by extension, RE, PSHE or geography) alive. Creative writing, in the form of poetry in particular, provided an exciting, involving and enjoyable avenue. It internalised the information I wanted the children to absorb and they had great fun learning.

Poetry should not be ghettoised within the English subject barrier. It can enliven and enrich the entire curriculum, give it relief and texture.

To summarise, a huge part, for good or ill, of what I am, has come from the poems I have read and the song lyrics to which I have listened. I wanted my pupils to have the chance to share that enjoyment, that process of spiritual and moral growth that can come through literature. One way of doing this was to get children to listen to, read and write poetry.

What kind of poetry should I write?

Over the years there have been many debates among writers and teachers about how to teach young people to write. A lot of this discussion breaks down into a tension between prescription and creativity. Some argue that we concentrate on the establishing of skills such as grammar, syntax, vocabulary, spelling and the various elements that can be taught: rhyme, verse, metaphor and simile for example. On this basis, the children will learn to use well-crafted forms to express their ideas. Their opponents respond that, yes, it is important to communicate the essential skills of the writer but the heart of the matter is their individual voice. How can he or she put over their own ideas, not those of the teacher or the text book? From this point of view, creativity comes before technique, individuality before correctness.

In my opinion, what really matters is the extent to which form is put at the service of the child's imagination and need to express himself or herself. One example most teachers will recognise of form getting in the way of self-expression is when children force everything to rhyme and end up with a sterile piece of doggerel. On the other hand, without some understanding of the poetic devices available to the young writer, classroom writing can become shapeless and ineffective. For the classroom teacher an intelligent synthesis of skills and creative self-expression seems the best solution.

Poetry covers a wide spectrum. There is, at one end, the more structured work focusing on what has generally been accepted as verse: rhymes, couplets, metaphors, carefully selected line breaks and repetition. At the other end you will find free writing, duplicating the rhythms of human speech. This is the poetry of direct statement. It aspires to being a more natural idiom than other, self-consciously poetic, forms. For twenty years I have been using both ends of this spectrum with children, for a couple of reasons really. Firstly, I think I am duty bound to reflect all strands of poetry to the children with whom I work, permitting them to investigate the merits of each and decide for themselves. Secondly, I work within the constraints of a national curriculum which prescribes what is to be taught, and both strands of poem are there. The point

8

of principle is not whether you work with the children on technique-based or free forms, but the extent to which it is *their* ideas, not yours, you are seeking to explore. Here is my brief attempt at a definition of the two strands.

Teaching technique-based or formal poetry

This is when the teacher uses the work of a poet found in a published book and asks them to write like that, in verse or nonsense, ballad or narrative, haiku or tanka, cinquain or clerihew. This is the approach commonly associated with Sandy Brownjohn in her books *Does it Have to Rhyme?* and *To Rhyme or Not To Rhyme?*

'The best way I have found of helping teachers overcome this problem [of lacking confidence in teaching poetry],' Sandy Brownjohn writes, 'because it was the way I found for myself, is to break the subject down into small, easily assimilated parts; each is one idea, one technique or one form. In other words, I separate all the individual details which go to make the whole.'

In her book, Brownjohn publishes some excellent work by young people. There is plenty of evidence of both self-discipline and imagination. She demonstrates practically how a particular form can give the children a ready-made framework.

To take one example, Brownjohn explores a simple conceit, poems about colour. A less assured practitioner would produce something like this:

> Blue is the sea.
> Blue is the sky.
> *Etc.*

The result is flat, dull and predictable, instant poetry of the worst kind. By developing, through discussion with the children, the idea that the colour should only be mentioned in the title, and by encouraging them to write about things a particular colour makes them think about, she achieves excellent results. Here is one:

Black

Else Thompson

> The old mine degenerating in the dead of night,
> The exposed body lying helplessly on the ground,
> An engulfing darkness in a maze of winding passages,
> The dagger of evil stained with blood,
> A cold and lingering silence.

(from *To Rhyme or Not To Rhyme*, p. 65.)

On the basis of this approach Brownjohn argues thus: 'We set the framework and provide the back-up while guiding the children towards their own autonomy.'

In an important comment, she also supports the idea of teachers 'having a go' themselves:

> 'I believe teachers should try writing themselves so that they know what to expect and can present the task sympathetically.'

I think this has a lot to commend it. In order to make an informed choice over which forms to exploit or even subvert, young writers need to explore how they work, to explore and adapt them. There is a potential downside. If teachers model everything, structure everything, they narrow the focus of what is possible. They close off young people's opportunities to express themselves. If, however, they go through a process of deconstruction then reconstruction with their pupils, they can put them in command of the forms and make them a route to self-expression.

Teaching free verse

I'll let Michael Rosen give this definition: 'Free verse is a way of writing things down in a way that helps someone to read it in the way you want them to. It is a kind of musical notation.'

Rosen, one of the trailblazers of exciting creative writing approaches in schools, argues that: 'We need to find forms that *release* children's knowledge, liberate it and so give the child a sense of his or her own power.'

What is key here is the use of line length to capture the rhythms of human speech, to make it natural, to be faithful to the content and meaning of what is being said. Here is an example:

I Was Naughty Once
Nicola Trew

One time when we were going to have dinner
Mum said will you lay the table please
And I said NO
Mum said
If
You
Don't
LAY
The table

You will not have dinner
Then dad came in
And said what is going on
Then I said I don't know Dad.

(from *Did I Hear You Write?* by Michael Rosen, p. 119).

One great virtue of this kind of writing is that it does not strain to be literary. It achieves a remarkable directness. Moments of the children's experience are valued and celebrated in writing. No subject is too small or too domestic for exploration.

Rosen concedes that 'there are times when it is appropriate to use a book-author's form and say to the children: You can write like that.' He then goes on to list the repertoire of forms children already have stored in their mental toolbox. It includes: 'rude rhymes, skipping rhymes, clap games, football chants, and for older children: rapping, toasting, country and western, rockabilly, soul, heavy metal and the whole gamut of pop forms.'

I suspect that these two poets would see their approach as being radically different. I have used both profitably, however. In the hands of an imaginative and charismatic teacher – and with the right training, support and time, most teachers can be both imaginative and charismatic – the formal is easily transcended. What's more, naturalness, the representation of human speech, can itself be a technique, and some of the poems quoted by Michael Rosen also have identifiable patterns within them that the young writer can assimilate and use.

The point is, there is no right or wrong in poetry. Teachers can profitably draw from the entire spectrum, the formal and the free. To get the best out of both many of the similar techniques will be used:

- *Demonstration and modelling*. The teacher writes sample versions of each section of the poem to support the young writer.
- *Brainstorming*. Asking the children to work in groups and share their ideas.
- *Sharing*. Reading parts of the poem in process out loud to focus the rest of the group on good practice.
- *Paired reading and revising*. Getting pairs of children to sympathetically review one another's work and make alterations.

It is important, above any other consideration, that we don't make the children's imagination subservient to the form. The form has to be put to the service of the child. He or she has to be the subject, not the object, of the learning process. How do you aid the child's intellectual development? Why, you do it with all the tools at your disposal. You do it by any means necessary.

Chapter 2

Some poetic forms to consider

In this section I have listed a few forms the teacher could introduce to the children to develop a repertoire. The aim of many is to encourage word play and mental agility. They could, for example, be used as a 'warm-up exercise' to encourage confidence and creative thinking. I have made no attempt to be exhaustive, simply to establish an approach and accumulate a usable resource, linked to the teaching framework used at present in British primary schools. Teach half of these and you will develop a varied and rich writing curriculum.

(*Note*: all unattributed poems are mine. They are included as resources for teachers.)

Some traditional English language forms

Nursery rhymes or traditional rhymes

One very productive area is to use traditional rhymes and create modern versions of them. There is a definite form to each of these rhymes which can be imitated. The children will find however that, once they have started, the task is more demanding than they thought. The process of writing entails vocabulary choices, additions and deletions, revision and redrafting. This is all good practice for the young writer. Here are some examples of traditional rhymes followed by their subversions.

Lucy Locket

Lucy Locket lost her pocket,
Kitty Fisher found it;
Not a penny was there in it,
Only ribbon round it.

The poem works through repeated sentence structures and rhymes. Another form which operates like this is the limerick. Here is my example of a subversion of the poem:

Lucy Locket

Lucy Locket wired a socket,
Kitty Fisher fused it;
Johnny Todd rubbed his eyes,
Girls are useless? Silly lies!

Here is another example of the traditional poem followed by its modern reworking.

There was a Little Girl

There was a little girl, and she had a little curl
Right in the middle of her forehead;
When she was good, she was very, very good,
But when she was bad she was horrid.

Again, rhyme and repetition makes the poem work.

There was a Little Boy

There was a little boy, and he had a frown
Right in the middle of his forehead;
When he was good, the teacher could win
But when he was bad how she needed a gin!

Working in this form is useful as an exercise. It also helps concentrate the mind of the young writer on the kind of message implicit in many traditional rhymes. It also encourages revision and redrafting. Omit or delete just one word and you fundamentally alter the rhythm of the whole.

An extension of this kind of activity might be for the children to read some of Roald Dahl's or Marian Swinger's poetic re-tellings of traditional tales and attempt their own versions (e.g. their poems on pp. 55 and 59 of *The Works*, edited by Paul Cookson).

Rhyme

Of all the questions young writers ask teachers, one of the commonest is that posed by Sandy Brownjohn in one of her books *Does it Have to Rhyme?* In her teaching Brownjohn went as far as to ban rhyme in the early lessons. It is easy to see why. There is nothing worse than forced or contrived rhymes. The less able child often ruins a piece of work by using rhymes which make no sense whatever. They even invent words until the poem loses all coherence. (*Note*: this is not a nonsense poem. Nonsense poems need a lot of intellectual agility and considerable skill to write. No, such a poem is just nonsense!) In my opinion, a poem is a delivery system for meaning. If rhyme gets in the way of this aim, then do away with rhyme. It is worth demonstrating rhyming couplets and rhyme patterns (ABAB, etc.) when they come up in the children's reading of poetry, but forcing poems to rhyme is usually counter-productive.

It is much better to introduce children to poems which use rhyme, near-rhyme and half-rhyme (terms which should be self-explanatory) and demonstrate how selective rhyme can work in a poem. Again, the excellent anthology *The Works* has sections on rhyme and rap, which explore the use of rhyme in a way which is accessible and fun. There are also two lessons on rhyme later in the book. Here is a poem which uses rhyme fairly loosely, in couplets and referring to rhymes several lines earlier:

Song of the Angry Child

I'm not going to do it,
listen to what I say,
no way,
no way!
You won't get me to read,
I don't see the need,
so let me be,
I just want to be free,
OK,
OK?
Lunch is a drag,
the teacher's a nag,
the kids are all pains,
they're all out of brains.
It's a terrible day,
A terrible day.
I won't play nice,
that breaks no ice.
I won't be good
like I promised I would.
What's the point?
What's the rotten point?
Because
no matter what I say
the other kids,
they all run away.
I don't know why,
Though it makes me cry
they
ALL
run away.

Here, on the other hand, is a poem with a stricter adherence to a rhyme pattern (ABAB):

January

Cataracts of mist form on the window pane,
Tears run in fine traceries on the glass
While evening, a dark, spreading stain,
Oozes between the streetlamps, a mass
Of greys, blues, blacks that colour you weary.

This poem uses a rhyming pattern before concluding with a pay-off line. This can be effective.

Acrostics

Read the first line of an acrostic downwards and it will form a word or phrase. A variation may be to write the key word down the middle of the poem. The acrostic, as a form, looks deceptively easy, but it requires some skill if the poem is not to sound contrived.

Homer

Heavy
Outsized
Man
Eating
Ravenously.

Fire

Flickering tongues lick
Into the inky night
Roaring itself hoarse,
Effervescent with flaring life.

Acrostics are particularly useful when writing about historical figures, seasons or celebrations. They are 'instant' poems and can be a very useful extension activity in various subjects.

Odes

Odes are, in Sandy Brownjohn's definition, 'lyrical poems generally employing exalted language to celebrate their subjects'. But, while odes worked for Keats, our modern age is less comfortable with the high, exaggerated seriousness of this form. Contemporary versions tend to work best by using incongruous subjects to create humour.

Ode to a Mobile Phone

Oh wondrous hand-held friend,
My constant companion,
My customised familiar,
How oft have you entertained me
With your ring tones, so musical, so sweet?
How many times have you alerted me
To a friend in need,
A snippet of gossip as tasty
As a super-sour dweeb?
Oh doorway to the outside world,
Oh photographer of pleasures,
Oh sender of texts,
Oh, provider of games,
How could I live without thee?
What would I ever do
With my restless fingers,
My ever-shortening attention span?

The more mundane, the more everyday the object (a bike, a dog, the school bell, the caretaker, a football team) the more opportunities there are for humour. The teacher simply has to demonstrate the various poetic conceits and devices. It is, incidentally, a good way to show, in context, how the exclamation mark and question mark work.

Thin poems

These are obviously poems, such as lists, in which there are only a few words on each line. The form can help deliver the ideas effectively. They also help focus the reader on the importance of the way the poem looks on the page. Presenting this poem on the left of the page will create a different response in the reader to centering it as below. The white space of the page to either side of the poem serves to emphasise its thinness. To be successful, there needs to be a synthesis of form and content. You probably wouldn't write a thin poem about a hippopotamus!

Diet

Mum
Hardly
Eats.
In
Fact,
She
Is
So
Thin,
If
You
Turn
This
Poem
Sideways
She
Will
Probably
Vanish.

Pin

Our
Teacher
Got
So mad
His
Head
Exploded.
You could
Hear
A pin
Drop.

Shape and concrete poems work according to similar rules. See *The Works* pp. 131 to 142 for examples.

Kennings

Kennings developed from the Anglo-Saxons' love of riddles. In this kind of poem you describe a thing without using its name. Usually you use a noun then an agent noun so an axe might be named *Blood letter*; a particularly wild-eyed teacher might be named *Pupil boiler*. The Kenning draws on the same skills as riddles. As an activity, Kenning-writing is good for developing mental dexterity. Kennings are ideal extension activities in history, geography, RE or PSHE. They are also much more fun and exciting than worksheets and demand more thought and invention.

Kenning

Wave skipper,
Ocean racer,
Earth strider,
Storm rider,
Head cleaver,
Blood bather,
Odin fearer,
Armour shearer,
Raven master.
Guess who?
A Viking.

Kenning

Face-twister,
Stair-stamper,
Computer-hogger,
Long-scowler,
Fridge prowler,
Spot-squeezer,
Sibling-teaser,
Sometime sulker,
Guess who?
Your teenage brother.

Cinquain

The cinquain, brainchild of the American poet Adelaide Crapsey, has 22 syllables, five lines and a sequence of 2, 4, 6, 8, 2. The last line often carries a sting in the tail.

It is similar to the haiku (see below). By creating a formula in which there is a specified number of syllables to each line, the poem demands intellectual discipline. For the young writer it also leads to reflections on line length, the shape of the poem, the choice of first and last line, sentence structure and other issues.

Batman Cinquain

Batman,
A lean machine
In his crime busting youth,
Eats so much junk food they call him
Fatman.

Clerihews

Clerihews are humorous four-line poems, named after their inventor, Edmund Clerihew Bentley, which usually give biographical details of a famous person.

They have a pattern of rhyming couplets: A, A, B, B.

Of course, there is no real reason why children have to be limited to biographical clerihews. The form would work equally well writing about places or topics.

Robin Hood
Was extremely good.
Those arrows of his he shot 'em
Where? Why straight at the sheriff's bottom!

Ann Boleyn grew rather thin
Trying to save her pure white skin.
She would have preferred to stay in bed
The day she went and lost her head.

Chants

Chants are rhythmic poems for one or more voices. Often they draw on an oral tradition. Because of the football associations these are often popular with boys. They work particularly well as performance poems or audience participation pieces. They can work very well in assemblies.

The Junk Food Chant

What do we want?
Burger and chips.
When do we want it?
Now!
What do we want it with?
Ketchup?
What will we wash it down with?
Fizzy drinks.
Then how will we feel?
Big and burpy.
How long will that last?
Until we puke.
How will we turn out?
Fat and pimply with rotten teeth.
How will that make us feel?
Really miserable.
Then what will we want?
Healthy food!
And when will we want it?
Forever!

Octopoems

Use this eight line formula, created by Australian teacher Christine Syme, to describe a person or topic. Like many of the ideas in this section, it gives the children a ready-made structure within which to explore their ideas.

1 A colour
2 A season
3 A place
4 A type of weather
5 A type of clothing
6 A piece of furniture
7 A TV show
8 A type of food

Octopoem

A teacher is amber.
She is the autumn,
A quiet village,
A breeze,
A cotton glove,
A comfy chair.
She is the latest news,
Your morning snack.

Some other world forms

Haiku

The Japanese poet Basho invented the haiku in the seventeenth century. The haiku was designed to evoke a picture in the mind, usually of nature.

The three line, seventeen syllable structure goes like this:
Line one: five syllables
Line two: seven syllables
Line three: five syllables.

This is a very good exercise for junior-aged children. It demands accuracy and concentration. It also challenges them to use a prescriptive form to develop an individual response. Strike a false note and you lose the emotional response of the reader.

An excellent way of presenting haiku is to write a couple around a similar subject, say Christmas. Put a line guide behind an A4 sheet of paper. Write one in the top, right-hand corner and the other in the bottom left-hand corner. Then put a border round each. In the two white spaces draw illustrations.

Christmas lights

Flickering brightly,
Tiny multi-coloured moths
Vibrate round my heart.

Snow

Like the crystal tears
Of an ice god, once bereaved,
They sting your red skin.

Combining these short poems with artwork is very effective.

Tanka

The tanka is another Japanese poem. Like the haiku it usually sums up a moment in nature, an image of one of the seasons.

The syllable pattern goes like this:
Line one: five syllables
Line two: seven syllables
Line three: five syllables
Line four: seven syllables
Line five: seven syllables.

Last Day in School

The streets are frozen
In remembrance of chatter.
The caretaker stands
With his scoop and bag sighing
Over the last crisp packet.

November 6th

Rain dimples the ash
Where fork-pierced potatoes baked
And tongues of flame danced
While rockets burst in showers
High above pointing fingers.

Free verse

Talk poems

Free verse works very effectively in reflecting human speech. By choosing line length, capitalisation and other techniques, the writer can develop insights into character and relationships.

Teacher and Me

My teacher,
that's MY teacher,
the one I'm stuck with,
not the one I choose,
you understand,
my teacher said:
sit up in your seat,

straighten your tie,
watch your capital letters
and
FULL STOPS,
don't look at me
in that
tone of voice
and
finally,
why oh why,
do you never
ever
SMILE?

Nightmare

So bad
I woke up crying.
So bad
I felt depressed all morning.
So bad
it left me
with a sick feeling
that put me off my dinner.
So
bad!

I wonder why I can't
Remember it.

In *Did I Hear You Write?* the children Michael Rosen works with come up with
such subjects as:
- mothers, fathers, sisters, brothers
- being sick
- going shopping
- Eid
- a squashed hedgehog
- days out
- bereavement.

It can be seen that free verse is a very versatile form which doesn't raise any formal barrier to the young writer. It simply demands that they explore their ideas and how to come up with a form for that exploration which is effective and readable.

Sentence poems

This is a variation on free verse. Write down a single sentence on a piece of paper then cut it up into line lengths whenever it sounds best. This works well when describing a moment in time, a memory, a dream, a nightmare. The cut up words pasted onto coloured paper or card also makes a good piece of work for display.

First day at school

With
My heart
In my mouth
I steered
My way
Through
The thirty-a-side
Football
To a corner
Where
I
Stood among
The
Crisp
Packets
Until
The whistle
Blew
Me
Into school.

You can experiment by rearranging the lines around the page.

My Dog

My
   dog
  ran
     like
        a
          mad
        thing
               all
                the
                   way
                     home
where
    he
      ate
        my sister's
               homework.
               Good dog!

Chapter 3

The lessons

Section 1: Lists

List poems are among the oldest and most effective forms of poetry. Many religious poems, for example, are lists of feelings, declarations, hopes, duties or rules.

Many children in school get used to poems such as Love is ... or *Liverpool is ....* Such poems are simple to write and, done with some originality, often achieve a resonance in the readers' or listeners' mind. Here's an example of a *That's Liverpool* poem. I don't make any great claims for it but it reflects this way of writing a poem.

That's Liverpool

A shudder of cold
From the Atlantic,
Grit dancing
On the M57 on a February morning,
Rubbish whipping round your legs
5pm Saturday afternoon
Great Homer Street market,
That's Liverpool.
A sun like a red-rimmed eye,
That's Liverpool.
Kwik Save carrier bags
Waving goodbye
To ghost ships,
Heritage trails
And cellophane-wrapped Beatles,
That's Liverpool too.
A snotty nosed kid
With a tear in her eye
And a spit of love
To wipe away the past,
That's Liverpool.

A poem like 'Me' shows how the list poem can be developed. The child could pick heroes or celebrities they would like to be and make a list of such people.

Me

Alan Gibbons

(with a nod in the direction of the sorely missed Adrian Henri)

Who would I like to be:
Michael Owen and David Beckham;
Arnold Schwarzenneger and Jean Claude Van Damme:
McCartney, Lennon,
Harrison or Starr,
With talent like that I could really go far.
Or maybe then,
I'd rather be:
Zinedine Zidane or Thierry Henry:
Ruud Van Nistelrooy or Stevie G;
Nelson Mandela or some other great fella
And, most definitely,
Last of all me.
Mind you, mulling it over,
Turning it round in my fertile mind,
Examining it carefully,
This way and that,
I quite like,
quite like,
Yes, really like …
ME!

Alternatively, they could make a list poem of the jobs they would like to do, places they would like to go. This latter idea could be incorporated into a geography topic. In history the children could list the people in the past they would like to have met, and why. If they added the reasons why they would develop the complexity and sophistication of the poem. In PSHE they might write about the values they hold dear. Even the youngest children are developing core beliefs. The opportunities are virtually endless, and the extent to which the child uses a structure derived from a poem to which they have been introduced, or works in a freer form, is entirely negotiable between the teacher and the class.

To do lists are an equally rewarding area for exploration. A poem such as 'Santa's To Do List' exploits a known area of activity and focuses the young writer on a list of phrases demonstrating what Santa has to do before the big day. Considerable humour can be produced by keeping the poem in Santa's voice.

Santa's To Do List

Feed the reindeer,
Tick.
Load the presents,
Tick.
Thank the elves,
Tick.
Grease the sleigh runners,
Tick.
Hang out the red suit,
Tick.
Polish the black boots,
Tick.
Stow the map and compass,
Tick.
Go to bed early,
Tick.
Set the alarm clock,
Tick
tock
Tick tock
Tick tock.

An extension of this might be a *Not to do* list, exploring the things your parents and teacher don't want you to do! For older children, a poem such as: 'A teenager goes shopping for life's necessities' could be interesting, asking the writer to explore where they think their life might go.

28

Lesson 1

Lesson Plan

Objective: discuss choice of words and phrases that create impact. Sentence punctuation and commas.

Stimulus: 'In a Naughty Kid's Pocket' by Alan Gibbons.

Sentence level: commas in a list.

Shared writing: demonstrate a simple list, then how to expand on one word items, using commas, parentheses, phrases.

Guided writing: 'Things You'd Find in a Bombed-out House'

In a Naughty Kid's Pocket
Alan Gibbons

In a naughty kid's pocket
you might find:
chewing gum
(at least three days old),
a burnt match,
a chewed bus ticket,
a felt tip pen,
a toenail,
a blood stain,
the teacher's patience,
a lock of blond hair,
a mouse –
dead obviously,
my pocket money.
That's what you'd
find in my brother's pocket.

Teaching the lesson

Shared writing

The teacher could begin by reading one or more list poems to the class. In this case the stimulus is a list of things found in a boy's pocket. The teacher could then introduce the idea of things found in a bombed-out house in World War Two (links to history topics are obvious). The lesson could start with the teacher scribing the children's ideas on the board, demonstrating commas in a list. With older children the addition of hyphenated phrases or parentheses might help to enrich the poem. The teacher can then discuss opening lines to help structure the poem and give a rough idea of the number of items to include and let the children explore.

Guided writing

While the children are working independently, having been shown how the poem works in the opening section of the lesson, the teacher can draw attention to the way poets re-draft. Can the children now look at their poems and decide which lines would work best at the beginning and which nearer the end? Why? Are there any phrases they wish to add? Do they want to play with rhyme? I always stress that poems do not have to rhyme and forced rhymes often ruin a poem. Rhyme, in order to work, has to add something to the poem, giving it rhythm and music, humour or insight. Finally, the teacher should choose a suitable moment to ask the children to look ahead to the end of the poem.

The young writer can then:
• choose one item which is particularly strong
• have a strong finishing off line to draw the poem together

Examples of children's work

Things You'd Find in a Bombed-out House

Daniel Brougham, Year 3

Here are some things you'd find
In a bombed out house:
Bits of blackened wood,
Shrapnel,
A smashed wireless,
Books,
A toy car,
Broken windows,
Smashed cups,
A ruined teddy.

Comments

The poem, interestingly, ends with a toy. This has an obvious emotional impact, suggesting perhaps the death of a child. With older children, the teacher could extend the poems by extending single words or short phrases into longer units of meaning. In this way, an older child might write:

Things You'd Find in a Bombed-out House

Here's what you might find
In a bombed out house:
Shrapnel,
Broken bricks,
Charred timbers exposed to the sky,
Shards of glass
Reflecting the splintered light of the sun,
Twisted metal,
Ashes dimpled with rain,
A smashed wireless –
Now quite dumb,
Its wiry tongue broken by a force
Stronger than words,
Books never to be read,
Broken ornaments,
A doll's head.

Extensions

Here are some further extensions to this basic idea:
• Ten things you'd find in Julius Caesar's pocket
• Ten new commandments for today
• Ten things I would really like to do
• Ten things I would really hate to do
• My ten worst nightmares
• My top ten favourite things
• Ten cunning plans

Lesson 2

Lesson Plan

Objective: to discuss choice of words and phrases that describe and create impact.

Stimulus: 'I Know Someone Who Can' by Michael Rosen.

Sentence level: the use of strong verbs in a sentence.

Shared writing: model things you can do on Rosen's text.

Guided writing: write their own version of 'I Know Someone Who Can'.

I Know Someone Who Can
Michael Rosen

I know someone who can
take a mouthful of custard and blow it
down their nose.
I know someone who can
make their ears wiggle.
I know someone who can
shake their cheeks so it sounds
like ducks quacking.
I know someone who can
throw peanuts in the air and catch them
in their mouth.
I know someone who can
balance a pile of 12 2p pieces on his elbow
and snatch his elbow from under them
and catch them.
I know someone who can
bend her thumb back to touch her wrist.
I know someone who can
crack his nose.
I know someone who can
say the alphabet backwards.
I know someone who can put their hands in
their armpits and blow raspberries.

I know someone who can
wiggle her little toe.
I know someone who can
lick the bottom of her chin.
I know someone who can
slide their top lip one way
and their bottom lip the other way,
and that someone is
ME.

Teaching the lesson

Shared writing

To introduce the lesson the teacher should read the poem with the class then discuss the structure Michael Rosen uses to deliver his ideas. This hinges, of course, on the repetition of *I know someone who can*. It is useful to write up a template of, say, four lines of 'I know someone who can' then ask the children to finish the sentences, e.g:

I know someone who can
Tidy her room.
I know someone who can
Do her times tables.
I know someone who can
Read two books a week.
I know someone who can
Dribble like Michael Owen.

Then ask: 'How many lines of poetry are there?' The answer, of course, is eight. Follow this with a second question: 'How many sentences are there?' The answer this time, hopefully, is four. By writing the sentence starter *I know someone who can* in one colour and the remainder of each sentence in a different colour the teacher can demonstrate the distinction between a line and a sentence and lead the children to think about the use of line length in poetry. Finally, in a third colour, the teacher can put in the punctuation. (In the plenary session at the end of the lesson there might be a further discussion about why some poets leave out the punctuation altogether.) In this way, fairly painlessly, and in context, the teacher is demonstrating sentence structure and line length.

If there are children with particular special needs in the class, it might be worth photocopying a number of lines starting: *I know someone who can*. This saves children who may be reluctant or unconfident writers having to toil through the secretarial task of writing down the repeated line. All they have to do is come up with their own ideas to complete each sentence. That, to me, is the point: to find a mechanism to get the children to write *their* ideas. What is gained by writing the words *I know someone who can* over and over again? Bart Simpson could manage that!

Guided writing

Having established the pattern of the poem we can now give the children several minutes to explore their ideas. In order to give a basic structure to the lesson it might be an idea to ask the children to start with one or two of the more realistic ideas, though this is voluntary, not obligatory. Can they think about the things they do that Mum or their teacher would like? In the second half of the lesson they can let their imaginations run riot.

Finally, having given them sufficient time to write down their ideas the children should be advised to look forward towards the end of the poem.

Michael Rosen completes his poem:

> 'And that someone
> Is me.'

It is worth modelling several alternative endings. For example, the children may want to insert an adjective to describe themselves, e.g.:

> 'And that wonderful someone
> Is me.'

Or maybe they prefer to write the whole poem in the character of, say, Dennis the Menace or Bart Simpson:

> 'And that terrible menace
> Is Bart Simpson.'

These are two of my suggestions. The children will probably come up with more of their own.

I Know Someone Who Can

Kristen Willoughby, Year 3

I know someone who can write neatly.
I know someone who can do handstands.
I know someone who can say their prayers.
I know someone who can climb Mount Everest.
I know someone who can ride a three wheel scooter.
I know someone who can hold their breath for 35 seconds.
And that little pest is … ME!

Someone

Jeffrey Chu, Year 3

I know someone who can
Sit on their bottom.
I know someone who can
Do their times tables.
I know someone who can
Make lanterns.
I know someone who can
Not mess on the carpet.
I know someone who can
Write a long story.
I know someone who
Can help someone in their house.
I know someone who can
Get on with their work.
And that someone is me.

I also know someone
Who can suck someone's blood.
I know someone who can
Kill the world's toughest man in the boxing ring.

I know someone who can
Pull their own teeth our with their hands.
I know someone who can
Go crazy.
And that cheeky someone
Is … Dennis the Menace!

I Know Someone Who Can

Gina, Year 4

I know someone who can
Do the dishes.
I know someone who can
Do their times tables.
I know someone who can
Tell the time.
I know someone who can
Make lanterns.
I know someone who can
Draw brilliant pictures.
I know someone who can
Tidy up their room (yeah, right!)
I know someone who can
Go up Mount Everest backwards.
I know someone who can
Throw socks in their air and eat them.
I know someone who can
Drink so much Coke it comes back out of their nose.
I know someone who can
Break the lead
Of a pencil and still use it.
And that beautifully mischievous menace
Is ME!

Comments

All three children exploit the simple structure successfully. Jeffrey shifts the focus of his poem in the second half to the character of Dennis the Menace. Gina adds an aside, using a parenthesis:

> 'I know someone who can
> tidy up their room (yeah, right!)

By doing so, she adds both texture and humour to the poem.

Extensions

Having established the basic structure of the poem, the teacher could successfully return to the format and extend it. If she read several puzzle poems or kennings to the class, asking them to guess the answer to the puzzle or to identify the subject of the kenning, she could then ask them to write a poem in the style of *I know someone who can* without identifying the subject of the poem. The plenary session of the lesson could consist of some of the children reading out their poems while the rest of the class tries to identify the character they are describing, e.g.:

I know someone who can

I know someone who can
Sit for years in a lonely old castle.
I know someone who can
Sleep in a coffin.
I know someone who can
Eat flies.
I know someone who can
Change into a bat.
I know someone who can
Stare into your soul.
I know someone who can
Drink blood.
And that demonic someone is ...?

Lesson 3

Lesson Plan

Objective: to write a poem with a repeated pattern.

Stimulus: 'Word of a Lie' by Jackie Kay.

Sentence level: consistent, coherent sentences.

Shared writing: demonstrating the pattern of the poem.

Guided writing: the children write their own versions of 'Word of a Lie'.

Word of a Lie

Jackie Kay

I am the fastest runner in the school and that's
NO WORD OF A LIE
I've got gold fillings in my teeth and that's
NO WORD OF A LIE
In my garden, I've got my own big bull and that's
NO WORD OF A LIE
I'm brilliant at giving my enemies grief and that's
NO WORD OF A LIE
I can multiply three billion and twenty-seven by nine billion
    four thousand and one in two seconds and that's
NO WORD OF A LIE
I can count the distance between planets before you've
    had toast and that's
NO WORD OF A LIE
I can always tell when my best pals boast and that's
NO WORD OF A LIE
I'd been round the world before I was three and a
    quarter and that's
NO WORD OF A LIE
I am definitely my mother's favourite daughter and that's
NO WORD OF A LIE
I am brilliant at fake laughter. I go Ha aha Ha ha ha and that's
NO WORD OF A LIE
I can tell the weather from one look at the sky and that's
NO WORD OF A LIE

I can predict disasters, floods, earthquakes and murders and that's
NO WORD OF A LIE
I can always tell when other people lie and that's
NO WORD OF A LIE
I can tell if someone is going to die and that's
NO WORD OF A LIE
I am the most popular girl in my entire school and that's
NO WORD OF A LIE
I know the golden rule, don't play the fool, don't boast, be
    shy and that's
NO WORD OF A LIE
I am sensitive, I listen, I have kind brown eyes and that's
NO WORD OF A LIE

You don't believe me do you?
ALL RIGHT, ALL RIGHT, ALL RIGHT
I am the biggest liar in my school and that's
NO WORD OF A LIE

Teaching the lesson

Shared writing

After reading the poem 'Word of a Lie' by Jackie Kay and enjoying its infectious chorus with the children, the teacher can scribe a few examples of sentences modelled on the poem. This time, whereas Michael Rosen's poem starts with the repeated line and concludes the sentence with an idea, Jackie Kay's begins with the idea then finishes with the repeated line:

> 'and that's
> NO WORD OF A LIE'

It is good for the children to see that poets can use a similar poetic device but vary how it is employed. This helps establish for the children a repertoire of skills from which they can draw in their own writing.

Guided writing

Once the children have explored the ideas collectively in class discussion they can go off and explore for themselves. At a chosen point the teacher can intervene and demonstrate how Jackie Kay herself concludes the poem. The children may well come up with alternative conclusions. It is the teacher's job to demonstrate just how the poet achieves her effects. The children can try duplicating them or coming up with similar ones of their own.

No Word of a Lie

Sean McLoughlin

I can eat a full banana in one second and that's
NO WORD OF A LIE.
I can kick a ball to Mars and that's
NO WORD OF A LIE.
My auntie lives in Buckingham Palace and that's
NO WORD OF A LIE.
My granddad is a thousand years old and that's
NO WORD OF A LIE.
I'm married to Kim Marsh and that's
NO WORD OF A LIE.
I've got longer hair than Rapunzel and that's
NO WORD OF A LIE.
I can run from England to Spain and that's
NO WORD OF A LIE.
I won 'Stars in their Eyes Kids' and that's
NO WORD OF A LIE.
I can jump into the sky and that's
NO WORD OF A LIE.
You don't believe me, do you?
ALL RIGHT, ALL RIGHT, ALL RIGHT!
I am the biggest liar in the world and that's
NO WORD OF A LIE!

No Word of a Lie

Meghan Bruder

I've had a number one in the charts and that's
NO WORD OF A LIE.
I'm the daughter of Victoria Beckham and that's
NO WORD OF A LIE.
I can climb the Eiffel Tower and that's
NO WORD OF A LIE.
I can read twenty books in two minutes and that's
NO WORD OF A LIE.
I have a dolphin in a Jacuzzi and that's
NO WORD OF A LIE.
Hilary Duff is my sister and that's
NO WORD OF A LIE.
I've been up to space four times before I was two and that's
NO WORD OF A LIE.
I have the darkest eyes in the whole of England and that's
NO WORD OF A LIE.
You don't believe me, do you?
All right, all right, all right!
I'm the biggest liar in the world and that's
NO WORD OF A LIE!

Comments

The structure of Jackie Kay's poem has given Meghan and Sean the confidence and the tools to investigate their ideas. The poems work very well, principally because the structure is so clear and easy to adapt. A good teaching point is to demonstrate the three kinds of sentence used by Jackie Kay. There are statements, questions and exclamations. Furthermore, there is the repeated use of the contraction *that's* for *that is*. Because the poem is fun and explores a familiar conceit it succeeds on many levels. For the teacher it lets the children use their imaginations, and incidentally demonstrates points of punctuation and grammar in context. That these points are in evidence over and over again because of the use of repetition is a boon. The point is not to produce hundreds of Jackie Kay poems but to get the children to understand how they can use various poetic devices in a poem.

Lesson 4

Lesson Plan

Objective: to explore a poem with a repeated pattern.

Stimulus: Christmas cards.

Sentence level: use of the colon to introduce a list.

Shared writing: demonstrate the structure using the repeated phrase to introduce lists of Christmas things.

Guided writing: children write their own poem: 'What Makes Christmas Special'.

Teaching the lesson

Shared writing

Discuss the idea of Christmas with the children. Lay out Christmas cards on the tables and ask the children to brainstorm Christmas ideas in group. After about ten minutes bring them back together and demonstrate the pattern of the first verse. First write up the opening line:

'At Christmas time I see:'

Now write the colon in a different colour and explain its use. The colon is the creative midfield player of punctuation. It is Paul Scholes, Zinedine Zidane, David Beckham. It sets up the play for the striker.

Finally, list the ideas the children have come up with. Encourage them not to give an item as a single word but a phrase employing a verb.

Guided writing

Once the youngsters are familiar with the structure of the verses, opening line then, for example, three ideas to a verse, the teacher can set them to work.

The opening of each verse changes. In order, it goes:

- At Christmastime I see:
- At Christmastime I hear:
- At Christmastime I smell:
- At Christmastime I taste:
- At Christmastime I feel:

It is a good teaching strategy to get them to write just one verse to begin with. Choose a few good examples and ask the authors to read out their opening verse. On the basis of this the teacher can decide how far to let the children go. Write two verses and share seems a reasonable way to proceed. In this way the lesson would break down into three phases. The final verse should look to tie up all the ideas.

Examples of children's work

What Makes Christmas Special

Samantha Regan

At Christmas time I see:
Glittering lights glowing in the grey sky,
Icicles dropping on the soft snow,
People putting shiny decorations on the tree.

At Christmas time I hear:
People cheering,
Children singing,
Hot milk boiling.

At Christmas time I smell:
Freezing snow twinkling on the ground,
Warm turkey cooking in the oven,
Fizzy shandy popping.

At Christmas time I taste:
Sizzling sausages,
Wonderful warm tea,
Hot mince pies.

At Christmas time I feel:
Soft cuddly toys,
Cheerful jolly Santa's beard,
Excited and happy!

Comments

The poem works as a very readable, atmospheric piece of writing. In this context, the punctuation makes sense. Exercises to teach punctuation are all well and good, so long as they are short and fun, but helping the children understand the use of the colon in the context of creative writing about a well-chosen subject means so much more to the child than writing a number of dull-as-ditch-water, decontextualised and utterly contrived sentences to teach a point.

Extensions

This structure would obviously work well with other festivals: Diwali, Eid, Hanukah or Chinese New Year. Seasonal poems could follow the same pattern. Places could be similarly celebrated.

Lesson 5

Lesson Plan

Objective: to write a poem using lists.

Stimulus: a discussion of the things people say.

Sentence level: colons, commas, semi-colons.

Shared writing: writing a first verse about memories.

Guided writing: children write a poem about memories, feelings and dreams, entitled 'My Life'.

Teaching the lesson

Shared writing

Based on a discussion of the children's memories, the teacher can demonstrate how to use an effective line, in this case *In the red box of memory* from the Verve song 'Sonnet', to introduce a list. Show how a colon introduces a list.

Guided writing

Having given the children a starter phrase, the teacher could also, before allowing them to begin writing, stress that when they write about the memory they could make it stronger by not just saying:

> 'My first Christmas at home.'

They could make it more resonant by adding what they saw, heard and so on during their first Christmas at home:

> 'My first Christmas at home
> Seeing the presents round the tree.'

By extending the phrase the writer can make the whole image more effective.

I would suggest allowing the children about ten or fifteen minutes to write the first verse, sharing some good examples, then showing two more starter lines:

> In the treasure chest of feelings
> I find …

> Finally, in the magic locket of dreams
> I find …

Each starter line leads into a new verse. All three verses should be of roughly the same length to give balance. Towards the end of the lesson the teacher can then brainstorm good quality endings.

Examples of children's work

My Life

Chelsey Hodgson

In the red box of memory
I find:
My first Christmas at home
Seeing my first toys and the colours
Blurring in my face;
My first day at nursery
Playing in the sand;
The day I got my dog
And it licked me on my face.

In the treasure chest of feelings
I find:
Joy at Christmas;
Love for my family;
Fun at a party with all my friends around;
Sadness when my granddad died;
Jealousy when my sister
Gets more money than I do.

Finally, in the magic locket of dreams
I find:
Me going to a college of forestry;
Me doing the crawl
Down my new swimming pool;
Me getting an Andrex dog.

There you go,
A life in three verses!

Comments

The effect of Chelsey's poem is very affecting. It reflects on loss and our personal feelings. It doesn't always show the writer in the best light, either, with Chelsey admitting to jealousy. The three part structure, followed by a strong closing line, give her the rein to explore emotion.

As with the other poems in this section, punctuation and grammar can be demonstrated in context. To sum up the lesson, there could be a discussion of alternative introductory lines which could be used to structure poems about personal experiences and aspirations.

Extensions

This kind of format would work well in describing an elderly person looking back at their life, maybe after inviting a grandparent or great-grandparent in to talk about their life.

Verse 1: 'When I was in the first flush of youth, I could: ...'
Verse 2: 'When I was fully grown, I could: ...'
Verse 3: 'Now I am old, I can: ...'

Section 2: Poems based on talk

Talk is the well-spring of writing. Story-telling, poetry and song all developed out of talk. Watch children bustling their way into school. What are they doing? That's right, they are making noise. But what kind of noise, I ask. They are telling stories. They are making up nonsense rhymes. They are asking one another riddles or telling jokes. They are singing popular lyrics. Most of all, they are playing with language, working out how best to communicate their identity and individuality to whichever of their peers they most want to impress.

Now teacher, listen to yourself. What do you do as you take your seats for in-service training? Are you really discussing the school development plan or making a learned critique of the government's latest educational initiative? Of course you're not. You too are telling jokes, stories, anecdotes. You are regurgitating last night's viewing to some poor unfortunate who missed the latest happening TV. You are humming some treasured snippet of song from years ago. Yes, there are places every one of us remembers all our lives. If you are male, you are probably testing somebody with a juicy bit of general knowledge or useless information. You might even be gossiping (interestingly, a recent newspaper survey reported that men gossip more than women). It's all talk and a lot of it good quality talk at that.

Good teaching is rooted in talk, immersed in it. What does the good teacher do? She interacts with the members of her audience, picks up their cues, entices them with anecdote, entertains them with humour. At her very best she makes the hairs on the back of their necks rise by logging on to their emotional hard-wiring.

Every word I write as an author resonates with echoes of the talk that has buzzed through the wires in my mind. I remember the anecdotes told by my family about all sorts of things: being scared by siblings dressing up as ghosts, keeping ferrets, finding a grass snake in the back yard on a country holiday. I remember my English teacher Mr Potts reminiscing about his wartime experiences and another English teacher, Mr Shaw, telling us how he went without shoes all summer.

Then there is the arena of great public talk. I remember Martin Luther King and his sublime 'I have a dream' speech. I remember Malcolm X encouraging people to fight back 'by any means necessary'. There are the recordings of Winston Churchill's speeches in the darkest days of the Second World War. There were the women trade unionists in the USA who wanted bread, but wanted roses too. There was Maya Angelou explaining how she knows why the caged bird sings. There were the words of Alan Bleasedale in the seminal TV drama *Boys from the Blackstuff*. Then there was Shakespeare, always Shakespeare.

So why not ask the children to write about talk? We are all immersed in it. We are all inspired by it.

We all do it.

Lesson 6

Lesson Plan

Objective: to write a list poem.

Stimulus: discussion of the things people say to each other.

Sentence level: the use of the colon, exclamation mark, question mark.

Shared writing: demonstrate an opening verse listing the things parents say.

Guided writing: children write a poem 'Talk' listing what parents, teachers and children say.

Teaching the lesson

Shared writing

The teacher could begin by asking the children to brainstorm all the things parents say. After bringing the children together, the teacher sorts some of the sentences they have drawn up into a list of phrases. She can then show how to open the poem with a simple introductory phrase such as:

Parents say:

She can also demonstrate how different kinds of sentence require different types of punctuation. She can use intonation to play a guessing game to determine which punctuation mark is most appropriate.

Guided writing

The opening phase of the lesson should explore what parents say. After hearing some good examples of children's work, the teacher can then write on the board the opening lines of the next two verses:

- Teachers say:

- Children say/We say:

She could point out different conventions. Some poets would plan all three verses to be of a reasonably similar length to give balance. Others would adopt a much freer style. Using her judgement she can then, at an appropriate moment, shift the children's attention to a good last line to tie up the poem.

Examples of children's work

Talk

Ellen Watts, Year 4

Parents say:
Your daddy is not going to come home yet.
Early night, madam!
These chocolates aren't for eating!
You are a little rascal!
Wash the floor, my little honey bunch.
Did you leave the shower on?
Get your homework sorted!
I'm getting angry!

Teachers say:
Wow! Look how much you've done! A merit mark!
No, you can't go to the toilet!
Less chatter! More work!
What is this supposed to say?
Oh, what is this? A love letter....to me!
How did this get here?

We say:

Oi! What are you doing here?

I want the Simpsons on.

Oi! Britney Spears was on then!

Tom! Stop it or I'll tell Mum.

But I don't want to do my homework!

Mum! Tom's teasing.

That movie was boss!

How does he do that?

Mum, I've chosen what hat I want.

That's what we say

(and parents and teachers!)

Comments

Ellen has a very acute ear for the way people speak. One of the things that makes writing a poem like this interesting is that the very art of writing is dependent, to a large extent, on accurately reproducing the rhythms and assonances of human speech. Punctuation, syntax and grammar in this instance are demonstrated by reading out loud. One enjoyable strategy is for the teacher to say sentences without words, just noises. The children can still hear which punctuation mark should match the sentence. They simply have to listen to the inflection of the teacher's voice. Speech can also be represented by line length: e.g.

'The teacher groaned

not

like

THAT!'

Extensions

An extension might be to explore how various famous people talk:

Talk

Cilla Black says: 'Surprise, Surprise';
Del Boy says: 'Cushty';
Victor Meldrew says: 'I don't believe it';
But Homer Simpson says:
'Doh, doh, doh.'

The Beatles say: 'Yeah, yeah, yeah';
The Black Sheep says: 'Bah, bah, bah';
Martin Luther King says: 'I have a dream';
But Homer Simpson says:
'Doh, doh, doh.'

The Queen says: 'One is not amused';
Tommy Cooper says: 'Just like that;
Terminator says: 'Hasta La Vista, baby';
But Homer Simpson still says:
'Doh, doh, doh.'

The opportunities, like human speech, are literally endless:
• things overheard at a football match
• overheard in the town centre on Saturday
• Mum says …
• Dad says …

Lesson 7

Lesson Plan

Objective: to write a poem in the form of a conversation between two people.

Stimulus: 'Conversation Piece' by Gareth Owen.

Sentence level: to secure a range of punctuation.

Shared writing: demonstrate an exchange between two people.

Guided writing: write a poem detailing a conversation between a teacher and a pupil.

Conversation Piece

Gareth Owen

Late again Blenkinsop?
What's the excuse this time?
Not my fault sir.
Whose fault is it then?
Grandma's sir.
Grandma's. What did she do?
She died sir.
Died?
She's seriously ill all right sir.
That makes four grandmothers this term
And all on PE days Blenkinsop.
I know. It's very upsetting sir.
How many grandmothers have you got Blenkinsop?
Grandmothers sir? None sir.
None?
All dead sir.
And what about yesterday Blenkinsop?
What about yesterday sir?
You missed maths.
That was the dentist sir.
The dentist died?
No sir. My teeth sir.
You missed the test Blenkinsop.

I'd been looking forward to it too sir.
Right, line up for PE.
Can't sir.
No such word as can't. Why can't you?
No kit sir.
Where is it?
Home sir.
What's it doing at home?
Not ironed, sir.
Couldn't you iron it?
Can't do it sir.
Why not?
My hand sir.
Who usually does it?
Grandma sir.
Why couldn't she do it?
Dead sir.

Teaching the lesson

Shared writing

After reading Gareth Owen's poem, a classic of its type, full of wry humour, the teacher asks how many voices there are in it. Once the children have identified that the poem works as an exchange between two voices, the teacher can begin to demonstrate how it works. The key to the poem is that the teacher poses a question. The child then answers it. This sets the pattern for the remainder of the poem. The teacher only needs scribe a couple of exchanges before asking the children to start work on their own poems.

Guided writing

Young children often need quite a lot of structure if they are to internalise patterns of language. By modelling the opening the teacher has established a template. The teacher can now ask the young writer to write an exchange between teacher and child over lateness.

The remaining verses, after sharing some good examples with the class, will concern the absence of a PE kit, missing homework and misbehaviour at playtime.

Finally, as usual, the teacher should ask the children to think carefully about the final few lines and how they can leave the reader with a satisfying conclusion to the poem.

Examples of children's work

Conversation (overhead in a school corridor)

Daniel Inwood

Late again, Daniel?
What's the excuse this time?
Car didn't start.
Lost my uniform and I had to go and get another one.
Elephant sat on my car.

No PE kit?
What's the excuse?
Dog went to the toilet on it.
A dinosaur stampede squashed the dog that was on my PE kit.
An earthquake swallowed up my kit.

Go on, tell me.
What's happened to your homework?
My dog ate it.
A pig rolled on my homework in the mud.
My mum threw it on the fire.

In trouble at playtime?
I do not believe it!
What now?
I accidentally karate chopped him in half.
I tried to shoot the wall, not Jimmy.

I am not Daniel.
I am a Mysteron replacement.

Comments

Daniel handles the duality of this piece of writing with complete confidence – and a lot of ironic humour. By putting this piece of work on an OHP the teacher can show how the punctuation of question and statement is intrinsic to the poem. In this way punctuation can start to make sense to the young learner, rather than being an imposition. It expresses something in the human voice and is part of the decoding of meaning. Punctuation can, in this way, be made organic to the process of writing, not some irritating addition at the end of it.

There are also some very mature touches. As an example, see how Daniel uses cumulative detail in Verse 2:

> 'Dog went to the toilet on it.
> A dinosaur stampede squashed the dog that was on my PE kit.'

Then there is the ending. It is very quirky, very individual and very successful.

Extensions

Take any double act and the young writer could turn the conversation into an effective poem. Think, for example, of the possibilities offered by:
- Batman and Robin argue about who is going to ask Cat woman for a date
- Julius Caesar's wife tries to persuade him not to go out on the Ides of March
- A row between Henry VIII and Ann Boleyn
- Cromwell and Charles I argue the rights and wrongs of the Civil War
- Churchill and Hitler debate the Second World War
- Harry Potter interviews Voldemort, asking where it all went wrong
- What Mum and Dad say when he's late home
- a phone conversation between you and Grandma

Lesson 8

Lesson Plan

Objective: to write a poem based on the way people talk.

Stimulus: discussion of the local dialects.

Sentence level: simple sentences.

Shared writing: use of a chorus to structure the poem. Spelling to reflect the accent in which the poem is spoken.

Guided writing: poem 'They do that, don't they?'

Teaching the lesson

Shared writing

The structure of this poem is simple. With the class, on the basis of a discussion of local dialect or phrases, the teacher chooses a chorus. In this case it is the Scouse: *De do dat, don't de?* Then it is simply a question of brainstorming local phrases and expressions and ordering them within the overall structure. The teacher should model a few lines before setting the children to work on their own poems.

Guided writing

Having established the structure, the core of the teaching is in releasing the children's knowledge of the way family and friends speak, reflecting the various elements of the local culture (in this case the north Merseyside town of Kirkby).

Examples of children's work

De Do Dat, Don't Dey?

Group poem, Overdale school, Kirkby

Me mam wears PJs to school.
Scousers: de do dat, don't dey?
Me da goes out on the ale.
Scousers: de do dat, don't dey?
Me sis nags me ma for money.

Scousers: de do dat, don't dey?
Me da snores of a night.
Scousers: de do dat, don't dey?
Me nan and gran shops in Netto.
Scousers: de do dat, don't dey?
Me and me bro ang around with Mancs.
Scousers: de do dat, don't dey?
Me unc goes down the betty then off to the offy.
Scousers: de do dat, don't dey?
Me n me crew go down to the chippy on a Saturday night.
Scousers: de do dat, don't dey?

Comments

There are pressure groups and certain national newspapers to whom any mention of local dialect is anathema. The idea that reflecting dialect, accent and local culture in children's writing involves some dumbing down of standards seems to me frankly ridiculous. Good teachers of English can simultaneously teach the skills in the standard English their pupils will require to compete in the world of work and also celebrate the richness of their spoken language. The children's poem is funny and inventive and stylised in its own way. Indeed, the question has to be asked: if they didn't have a good grasp of standard English, could they so effectively duplicate in recognisable spelling the conventions of the Liverpool accent? As an analogy, look how successfully many bi-lingual children operate. Moving from one code to another stimulates linguistic flexibility.

Extensions

A similar exercise could be repeated with just about any accent, patois or dialect.

A variation might be to write a conversation completely constructed of Elvis Presley or Beatles' lyrics – or the modern equivalent, something this writer doesn't feel equipped to explore!

Section 3 – Diary poems

I listed many sub-genres of poetry above. Here are a few more to consider:
- traditional rhymes
- nursery rhymes
- fables
- tongue twisters
- puns
- riddles
- prayers
- nonsense poems
- adverts
- letters
- raps
- couplets
- choral poems
- diaries

What the teacher can successfully do is to establish a repertoire of exciting and entertaining forms. Over time the child will have a series of delivery systems for their poems. A diary is one such delivery system and it can pack quite a punch. There is, for a start, an obvious structure, that being the seven days of the week. The two poems in this section both exploit this pattern.

Lesson 9

Football Training
Celia Warren

Monday
Practised heading the ball:
Missed it – nutted the neighbours' wall.

Tuesday
Perfected my sideline throw:
Fell in the mud – forgot to let go!

Wednesday
Worked in my penalty kick:
A real bruiser – my toe met a brick.

Thursday
Gained stamina – went for a jog:
Ran round in circles – lost in the fog!

Friday
Developed my tactical play:
Tackled the goal post – it got in the way.

Saturday
Exercised – twenty-eight press-ups:
Did pull a muscle – but no major mess-ups.

Sunday
At last – the day of the match!
Came through it all without a scratch.
The ref was amazed how I kept my nerve;
He agreed it's not easy to be the reserve!

Teaching the lesson

Shared writing

The children will have noticed, listening to the poem, that there is an obvious pattern:

> Monday,
>> did this ...
>
> Tuesday,
>> did this ...
>
> Wednesday,
>> did this ...

Scribing, the teacher can show on the board how to arrange the lines to duplicate the way she has read it, where to pause, how to represent the structure of the sentence. In passing, she could point out how the comma is used to stand for a breath or pause.

Guided writing

In order to get the best writing for the children, brainstorming ideas about Superman, what he does, where he is from, who his enemies are, might help. It is essential to develop a landscape of ideas.

This done, the teacher could ask them to write two or three entries before bringing the children together to hear some good examples. After this focus, she could return them to their desks to complete the next three verses, leaving only the final verse to discuss. Again, the purpose of this is to emphasise the importance of a good conclusion to a piece of writing, the need, as some of the cast of *Friends* might put it, to obtain closure.

Examples of children's work

Diary – Superman's Week

Mamie Dillon, Year 4

Monday,
I popped into a phone box
And changed.

Tuesday,
Saved a man from tripping
Over.

61

Wednesday,
Went to Asda and I took
1.5 seconds to do the shopping.

Thursday,
I saved a man from
Shooting a football.

Friday,
Stopped a stone from
Falling on a woman below.

Saturday,
Went on holiday to
Australia and flew there by myself.

Sunday,
I put my super feet up
And rested.

Comments

Mamie shows complete control of the diary form. There is a lot of humour in the poem, especially in the final verse. She uses the day of the week on a line on its own to emphasise it and a comma to tell the reader where to pause. This is a small point, but it helps the presentation of the poem. It is an accomplished piece of work.

Extensions

The diary form could be applied to any storybook character, historical figure, celebrity or religious figure. Try some of these:
• Julius Caesar's week, ending on the Ides of March
• Spiderman's week
• Lyra's week
• The Big Bad Wolf's week
• Ann Boleyn's week
• Theseus's week
• Captain's log for the *Titanic*
• Captain's log for the *Starship Enterprise*. (Star date 14,987 or some such might replace Monday, Tuesday.)
• Santa's week, leading up to Christmas Eve

Lesson 10

Lesson Plan

Objective: to use the diary form to write a dystopian poem.

Stimulus: 'Seven Days'. If you think this poem is too complex, use Jack Howarth's poem on p. 65.

Sentence level: role of verbs in sentences.

Shared writing: establishing a framework, an opening and a template for writing the poem.

Guided writing: complete a poem 'Seven Days', using the original as a model.

Seven Days
(dedicated to Edwin Muir)

Monday, the first day,
there was a fireflash
brighter than a thousand suns.
Tuesday,
grey dust settled everywhere,
choking us,
making living statues of everyone.
Wednesday and Thursday,
the TV screens
went blank,
the radios fell silent.
Friday,
the last streetlamp
flickered then died.
Nobody walked the streets.
Even the dogs remained indoors.
Saturday,
we huddled afraid in our homes.
Sunday,
the last day for some,
was the day we met

in the school hall
and swore that we would survive.
Now there is just one question:
how?

Teaching the lesson

Shared writing

After reading the poem, the diary of a week of destruction, the teacher can discuss with the class how to turn this into a poem. How does line length work? Should the day of the week be on a different line to show the reader where to pause for effect? What images will they use? What would have changed in their locality? How would they show that the world had fallen apart? They will be using the seven days of the Creation but invert it so as to reflect on the destruction of modern civilisation by some man-made disaster.

The teacher could model the events of the first two days to show the children how to get started.

Guided writing

Having established the tone of voice and the structure of the poem, the teacher can now set the children to work on their own poems. Again, scaffolding the lesson, asking the children to work on, say, the first four days, then getting several children to share what they have written, is a good strategy for focussing the whole class.

After a short intermission to share the ideas of the chosen group, the teacher can point out strong points and get the children to look forward to the rest of the poem. Using local landmarks helps make the impact more immediate. The teacher could perhaps point out how, in a film like *Deep Impact* or *Godzilla*, witnessing the destruction of familiar places like the Empire State Building intensifies the emotional impact of the story. In the case of this poem, we are effectively giving the children a ready-made opening and ending. Some of the more able children may want to come up with their own versions. It is the visual cues in the poem that carry the punch. It might be advisable to have some pictures of local landmarks on display to trigger the children's imagination.

The Horses

Jack Howarth

Barely a twelvemonth after
The seven days war
That put the world to sleep,
The horses came.
On the first day of the war
I saw Prescot church, once a huge cone,
Just broken bricks.
On the second day
The television went dead.
On the third day
All the ferries drifted past,
Covered with skeletons.
On the fourth day
I noticed there were no birds,
Just grey sky.
On the fifth day
I walked down to Liverpool.
I saw the cathedrals ruined
Down 'no hope' Street.
On the sixth day
I saw the Liver Birds crushed.
On the last day
The horses came.
Our life is changed,
Their coming, our beginning.

Comments ▉▉▉▉▉▉▉▉▉▉▉▉▉▉▉▉▉▉▉▉▉▉▉▉

Jack's poem comes from a similar idea. It was a response to the poem 'The Horses' by Edwin Muir. In the poem the world is destroyed by a nuclear explosion, leaving a handful of survivors bewildered and numb. Finally, a strange breed of horses arrives to help manking build a future less dependent on dangerous technologies.

Jack uses the diary form expertly. The poem's power is derived from a combination of Edwin Muir's evocative opening and ending and Jack's deceptively simple lines detailing the disintegration of modern society. For anyone who does not know Liverpool, the mention, on the fifth day of the cathedrals ruined down 'no hope' Street, refers to Hope Street which joins the Anglican and Metropolitan cathedrals. It is a very mature and striking line.

Hopefully, it is self-evident that, by writing a simple diary poem like 'Superman's Week' in Year 4 and a more complex one like 'The Horses' in Year 6, progression can be built into the English curriculum. The next stage for the pupil in High School would be to generate their own opening and closing lines in a similar project.

Extensions

Various dystopian visions could be explored using this basic model:
- The Earth endangered by a comet
- The Earth after its resources of fossil fuels ran out, what American writer Michael Moore has called 'The Big Die-in'
- A modern city after a biological attack

Section 4: Repeated lines

The use of repetition as a basic structure is as old as poetry and song. It remains, however, a tried and tested form through which to explore ideas.

Lesson 11

Lesson Plan

Objective: to use repeated lines in a poem.

Stimulus: 'Wings' by Pie Corbett.

Sentence level: writing coherent sentences, conditional verbs.

Shared writing: demonstration of *If ... I would* as the basic unit of the poem.

Guided writing: a poem 'If'.

Wings
Pie Corbett

If I had wings
   I would touch the fingertips of clouds
     and glide on the wind's breath.

If I had wings
   I would taste a chunk of the sun
     as hot as peppered curry.

If I had wings
   I would listen to the clouds of sheep bleat
     that graze on the blue.

If I had wings
   I would breathe deep and sniff
     the scent of raindrops.

If I had wings
   I would gaze at the people
     who cling to the earth's crust.

If I had wings
I would dream of
swimming the deserts
and walking the seas.

Teaching the lesson

Shared writing

Demonstrate how to structure the repeated lines:

'If I had wings,
I would ...'

Some children are unfamiliar with the conditional voice so it takes some oral explanation of how it is used. Further demonstrate how line length shows how to read the poem.

Guided writing

The lesson can be structured in three parts:
• If I had wings ...
• If I had fins ...
• If I had magic powers ...

This allows the teacher to bring pace to the lesson and to gather the children at regular intervals to share ideas. In summing up the poem the children could use the connective: finally.

Examples of children's work

If

Emma Walker

If I had wings
I would fly to Jupiter
And see the rocks like a grey sheet.

If I had wings
I would fly over the forest
And see the squirrels race.

If I had wings
I would fly to White Rose
And see the cars like spilt sweets.

If I had fins
I would swim to the French beach
And see the gold-finned mermaids playing by the sea.
If I had fins
I would travel to the depths of the ocean
And hear the whales sing.

If I had fins
I would swim to the Atlantic
And see the penguins toboggan.

Finally, if I had magic powers
I would be an animal
To see the other animals.

If

Rebecca Winters

If I had wings
I would travel to Alton Towers
And see the wonderful rides.

If I had wings
I would travel over the seas
And see all the glittering water gleaming.

If I had fins
I would swim to Florida
And see Minnie Mouse.

If I had fins
I would travel to the bottom of the sea
And see all the starfish.

Finally, if I had magic powers
I would have a holiday every day
And see all the wonderful sights.

Comments

As we have seen earlier, armed with a simple but effective structure, junior-aged children can write fluently and imaginatively. Both young writers responded to the stimulus individually. After watching the adult modelling how to write a clear, effective sentence, they had the tools to express themselves.

Extensions

There are many other such repeated lines in song and poetry. Here is just one to try, from 'El Condor Pasa' by Simon and Garfunkel. The repeated line here is:

> 'I'd rather be a hammer than a nail,
> Yes I would, if I could,
> I surely would.'

It is a structure that can easily be used by pupils to write evocative poetry. Simplicity can be more powerful than artifice.

Section 5: Using rhyme

One of the most common questions put to teachers, poets and authors in writing lessons is, as I pointed out above: 'Does it have to rhyme?' The answer, of course, is no. Many poems make no attempt to rhyme. What's more, some of the more clumsy attempts at rhyme make young people's work stilted and contrived. My usual answer to the perennial question about rhyme is: 'Only if it makes the poem better. If in doubt, leave it out.'

Intelligent use of rhyme can of course add considerably to the rhythm and musicality of a poem, so here are two ideas which I have found to work.

Lesson 12

Lesson Plan

Objective: to write a poem employing rhyming couplets.

Stimulus: the poem 'Song of the Homeworkers' from Paul Cookson's anthology *Unzip Your Lips*.

Sentence level: use of rhyme.

Shared writing: demonstrating how rhyming couplets work.

Guided writing: writing a poem 'Song of the School Workers'.

Song of the Homeworkers
Trevor Millum

Homework, moanwork
Cross it out and groanwork.

Homework, neat work
Keep you off the street work.

Homework, moanwork
Cross it out and groanwork.

Homework, roughwork
When you've had enough work.

Homework, moanwork
Cross it out and groanwork.

Homework, dronework
Do it on your own work.

Homework, moanwork
Cross it out and groanwork.

Homework, gloomwork
Gaze around the room work.

Homework, moanwork
Cross it out and groanwork.

Homework, guesswork
Book is in a mess work.

Homework, moanwork
Cross it out and groanwork.

Homework, rushwork
Do it on the bus work.

Homework, moanwork
Cross it out and groanwork.

Homework, hatework
Hand your book in late work.

Homework, moanwork
Cross it out and groan g r o a n GROANWORK!

Teaching the lesson

Shared writing

The teacher starts by reading the poem. Immediately the children will pick up the lively rhythm of the poem. The teacher can then ask the children what makes it work. That it involves rhyme soon emerges from discussion. The teacher can then send the children off to explore rhymes related to the word *school*. The rhyming pattern of this poem is very specific, emerging from the one word. By writing up several lines in one colour pen and inserting rhymes in a different colour the teacher can establish how the rhyme scheme works. She will also need to do some work beating out syllables to show how the rhythm is created.

Guided writing

On the basis of lots of exploration of rhyme and rhythm, the teacher can then set the children to work. As above, I find that limiting the children to a few lines to begin with works best. If any of them are losing the plot, reading some examples of good practice, scribing them on the board or putting them up on an OHP helps focus the children in the class who are finding the task difficult. Writing rhyming poems in particular often takes a lot of re-drafting. It should be pointed out that crossing out is fine. It takes time to find the best words. You also have to do lots of deleting and adding in order to get the rhythm right.

In the second phase of the lesson, building on the foundation of the first section, the teacher can then direct the writers' attentions to the final line when you need to bring it to a conclusion. Modelling a number of suggestions helps fix the objective in the children's minds.

Examples of children's work

Song of the School Workers

Jessica Bennett

School work, fool work
Put it in the bin work.
School work, gruel work,
Can't be bothered work.
School work, cruel work,
Want to go to bed work.
School work, pool work,
Water in your ears work.
Want to watch the telly work.
Definitely not cool work.

Comments

Jessica has used the format extremely confidently. Rhythm and rhyme both contribute to an effective final product and the final line pulls it all together. As a performance poem, this works perfectly.

There are numerous outlets for rhyming poems. One which works particularly well is a poem based on *My Cat Likes to Live in Boxes* by Lynley Dodd. The children could base a poem on Dodd's picture book changing the place names Paris, Berlin, etc. to ones in their locality.

My Cat Likes to Live in Boxes

The cat from Crewe
Has got the flu;
The cat from Kirkby
Plays with his furby;
The cat from Speke
Feels rather weak
But my cat likes to hide in boxes.

The cat from St Helens
Likes the taste of melons;
The cat from Liverpool
Is really very cool;
The cat from Chester
Well, he likes to pester
But my cat
Likes to hide in boxes.

A similar idea based on historical figures might similarly generate some interesting ideas:

Julius Caesar hid in the freezer;
The feet of Isambard Kingdom Brunel
Didn't half smell ...

This kind of wordplay is fun for the children and helps enrich their language. Raps are another obvious area for exploration of rhyme.

Lesson 13

Lesson Plan

Objective: to produce revised poems for reading out individually.

Stimulus: 'My Granny is a Sumo Wrestler' by Gareth Owen.

Sentence level: how meaning is affected by the structure and sequence of clauses.

Shared writing: 'My Granny is a Lion Tamer'.

Guided writing: poem about a Granny who has a similarly incongruous job.

My Granny is a Sumo Wrestler
Gareth Owen

My granny is six foot three
My granny is built like a tree
My granny says – *Nothing*
I mean nothing
Frightens me.

When granny walks down the streets
She scares every man she meets
Nobody gonna mess with her
My granny is a Sumo Wrestler.

My granny is six foot three
My granny she's built like a tree
My granny says – *Nothing*
I mean nothing
Frightens me.

My granny she does what she likes
My granny rides two motorbikes (at the same time)
My granny she breaks down doors
My granny bends bars with her jaws.

My granny is six foot three (that's sitting down)
My granny she's built like a tree
My granny says – *Nothing*
Absolutely nothing
Frightens me.

75

My granny is a railway ganger
My granny is a wild head banger
My granny eats uncooked bison
My granny beat up Mike Tyson (in the first round).

My granny she's six foot three
My granny she's built like a tree (oak tree)
My granny says – *Nothing*
And I mean nothing
Ever
    Ever
      Ever
        Frightens me.

Teaching the lesson

Shared writing

A good way of introducing this poem is using an interactive whiteboard. Highlight the repeated lines in the poem which give it its structure e.g.:

> 'My Granny says nothing,
> I mean nothing,
> Frightens me.'

Demonstrate how the repetition of these lines and the variations upon them work. They are the skeleton on which the flesh of the poem is laid. Once this structure is in place, the children, in order to write their own versions, can explore the rhyming couplets which complete the poem.

The teacher, through discussion, could demonstrate the kind of rhymes which work, starting with the opening lines. Gareth Owen has used the words 'six foot three' to get his rhyme. The children could use six foot one, six foot two, six foot four, six foot five, etc. and find a rhyme. The rest of the poem consists of rhymes based on Granny's unusual job.

Guided writing

Once the underlying structure of the poem has been established, the teacher can concentrate on drawing out rhymes that work. The job the children choose should be suitably macho, the incongruity of lion tamer or deep sea diver with the standard image of the granny offering plenty of scope for humour. As usual, sharing good examples works. Reading out loud helps focus the mind on rhythm and on the use of line length to replicate the human voice. Gareth Owen's poem is wonderfully performable. The children should be under no pressure to produce a finished product in one session. The process of re-drafting, revision, addition and deletion helps give the final version polish. All authors are continually re-reading and re-working their texts.

Examples of children's work

Granny is a Belly Dancer

Jemma Halfpenny, Year 6

My granny is six foot eight,
My granny has got no mates.
My granny says nothing,
I mean nothing
Frightens me.
My granny, she shakes her hips
My granny has red juicy lips.
My granny says nothing,
I mean nothing,
Frightens me.
My granny has got a big belly,
My granny eats lots of jelly.
My granny says nothing,
Ever, ever, ever
Frightens me!

My Granny is a Rugby Player

Dominic O'Neill

My granny is six foot two,
She's built like an angry Zulu.
My granny says:
Nothing,
I mean nothing,
Frightens me.
My granny is so tall!
With a flick she knocked down

My garden wall.
My granny is a rugby player.
My granny burst the Ozone layer.
My granny says:
Nothing,
I mean nothing,
Frightens me.
My granny, she likes to win.
My granny is an idolised kingpin.
My granny can conquer the world
(That's what she thinks).
My granny is a rugby player.

Comments

Both poems mine a rich vein of humour. They are linguistically inventive and exploit the rhythm of the poem very confidently. Moreover, they are very individual and inventive. I would certainly never, in a month of Sundays, have expected Dominic's idea of:

'My granny is an idolised kingpin.'

It is one of the pleasures of the English teacher that, even when the whole class are responding to the same stimulus, each individual writer comes up with a totally different response.

Extensions

The list of weird and wonderful jobs Granny could do is virtually endless:
• lion tamer
• deep sea diver
• mountain climber
• champion steeplejack
• heavyweight boxer
• private detective
• Formula One driver
• TT biker

Using Gareth Owen's poem as a template can help the children understand how several elements combine to make this poem work. Perhaps they will later be able to exploit this and generate something original of their own using the insight.

Section 6: Nature poems

Nature poems form a significant sub-genre. Many of our best-loved poems feature nature. Just think of Wordsworth's 'Daffodils', Blake's 'Tyger', Ted Hughes' 'Hawk in the Rain'. Nature provides a fertile area for exploration. Nor is it just a matter of description. There is often great drama in scenes from nature. I was speaking recently to a teenage audience in Lewisham, south London when I noticed, out of the corner of my eye, a fox rummaging in a bin. Analogies with other, human, foragers spring immediately to mind, and that is an important point. Nature poetry does not have to hark back to some iconic rural past. It can make us reflect on all kinds of perennial or modern human behaviour. Then there is the whole area of the kill, witnessing a predator in pursuit of prey. Again, it doesn't take a huge leap of the imagination to see how this focuses the mind on some of the worst aspects of human behaviour. Anyone who has watched the brutish, desperate struggle of the German and Jewish-American soldiers in *Saving Private Ryan* will be reminded, with its screams and grunts of pain, of the primal struggles of wild creatures.

Teachers should take care not to select exclusively from European and American poetry. Some of the greatest nature poems have emerged from the oral traditions of African society. In Ted Hughes' and Seamus Heaney's collection *The Rattle Bag* there is a wonderful series of Yoruba poems. It is hardly surprising that wordsmiths from societies with a much greater proximity to nature than modern industrial societies have produced some of the most stunning responses to the animal world.

Children, even in the most urban areas, can benefit hugely from exploring nature.

Lesson 14

Kob Antelope

Anon (translator Ulli Beier)

A creature to pet and spoil
like a child.
Smooth-skinned
stepping cautiously
in the lemon grass.
Round and plump
like a newly married wife.
The neck
heavy with brass rings.
The eyes
gentle like a bird's.
The head
beautiful like carved wood.
When you suddenly escape
you spread fine dust
like a butterfly
shaking its wings.
Your neck seems long,
so very long
to the greedy hunter.

Leopard

Anon (translator Ulli Beier)

Gentle hunter
his tail plays on the ground
while he crushes the skull.

Beautiful death
who puts on a spotted robe
when he goes to his victim.

Playful killer
whose loving embrace
splits the antelope's heart.

Teaching the lesson

Shared writing

Read the pair of Yoruba poems entitled 'Kob Antelope' and 'Leopard'. Discuss with the children how the poet uses contrasting imagery for predator and prey. Discuss also the surprising imagery in 'Leopard' which is reminiscent of numerous movie vampires and their victims. Finally, suggest bringing together predator and prey in a single poem. The pattern of many movies is useful. It goes something like this:

Man walking along the street. He hears a noise.
A following figure shrinks into the shadows.
The man looks back for a while then continues.
The footsteps resume behind him. He looks back again.
The silhouetted figure stops.
The man starts to run. He turns a corner. A knife flashes.

This is a well worn technique but it can be used. A pattern of prey, predator, prey, predator, kill, works well in a nature poem. Any creatures could be used. In this case we will have a hawk and a mouse. Having established the structure the teacher can demonstrate how to get the poem started with a striking opening line, using a subordinate clause to create resonance.

Out on the grass,
Under clear skies,
There was a mouse.

We will return to this opening later in a circular pattern. The teacher could finally brainstorm ideas about the mouse. A labelled diagram is a useful stimulus. It helps, among other things, to establish the vocabulary available to the young writer. Many of my pupils on the eastern rim of Merseyside didn't know the word 'talon'. Indeed, some did not know what a badger or hedgehog was. Having explored the area of vocabulary, the teacher could then model a couple of lines, e.g.:

> Its fur was silver grey.
> It ruffled in the morning breeze.

The effect is produced because of the contrast between the soft, vulnerable mouse and the savage, merciless hawk. Contrasts work well in this kind of poem.

Guided writing

The teacher can now ask the children to explore how the mouse moves. Does it scurry, scamper, scuttle? Why do these words all begin with *sc-*? Does the mouse look out for danger? Which senses does it use? What similes can we use to describe its features? Now share some of the first verses the children have written.

Next examine the labelled diagram of the hawk. How can we describe it, contrasting it to the mouse? How does a hawk fly when it is looking for prey? Does it hover, glide, swoop, plummet?

Return to the opening line, referring back to it, e.g.:

> Out above the grass, under those self-same cruel skies,
> There was a hawk.

Again the children explore the creature. Finally, to conclude the poem, discuss the kill. The analogy of the penalty taker is useful. Just think how, in a big match, seventy thousand people can fall into a hushed silence just before the ball hits the net and there is an explosion of sound. Much the same pattern of the quiet before the storm often applies to a predator taking down its prey. Stress the importance of the last line and how it needs to be evocative, leaving the reader with a sense of resolution.

The Kill

Emma Moulsdale, Year 7

Out on the grass,
Under clear skies,
There was a mouse.
Its teeth were nibbling tiny seeds.
Its nose was twitching.
Its tail was darting across acres of grass.
The mouse sniffed for danger.

Out above the grass, under those cruel skies,
There was a hawk.
Its eyes were cold as stone.
Its feathers ruffled in the breeze.
Its beak was ready to catch its prey.

That's when silence entered the earth.
A dart of feather and flesh cut crystal air.
The hawk becomes a missile.
The hawk hits its victim
Like a tree falling to the ground.
The tiny creature shudders then is still.

Flesh of the mouse scattered
Across the talons of the hawk.
Blood sprays around like a squirt of perfume.
The hawk bathes in her blood.

The Kill

Scott Vickers, Year 6

The mouse
Munching seeds
Playing in the grass
Glad to be alive.

The python
Tasting the air,
Slowly moving up the rock,
Its forked tongue flickering.

The mouse
Silent
Still
Alarmed at danger.

The python
Waiting…
SMACK!!
Constricts the mouse.

The mouse
Like a broken bone
Flopping about
Knows it's lost.

The python
Stretches its jaw,
Eats the mouse,
Digests his prey.

Then slowly moves off.

Hare

Kelly Farrell, Year 8

Swift runner,
I see you, snaking through the tapering grass,
Weaving and darting
In the drops of yellow gorse.

Lithe sprinter.
The sun strokes your back with its gentle fingers
And the fragrant grass ripples and parts
As you pass.
Stop!
The world shudders to a halt!
Your fearful nemesis awaits
Unfurling its black wings
In the final crucifixion.

Comments

In all of these poems the young writers show a growing command of structure, description and dramatic effect. There are some striking images: Emma's 'blood … like a squirt of perfume'; Scott's 'mouse like a broken bone flopping about'; Kelly's 'final crucifixion.' Form and content fuse, complementing one another in a satisfying synthesis.

Extensions

There are many striking variations on the predator and prey theme:
• the spider closing on the fly stuck in its web
• the lion stalking a zebra
• the crocodile snapping up an unwary wildebeest

A further extension would be to extend the scenario to a commando stalking a sentry in a jungle. Empathy with the victim could be generated by focusing on a letter or photograph from home. In the final poem the treasured object could be spotted with blood or trampled in the mud. All too often, violence on TV is both graphic and devoid of emotional impact. In depicting violence, teachers should never forget the cost to the victim. By individualising the victim we stress empathy. Empathy, the ability to walk in the shoes of another human being, is one of the most vital of values.

Section 7: Place poems

Living in Liverpool, an indisputably charismatic city, I am attracted to writing about places. Apocryphally, Jon Anderson, lead singer of the rock group Yes, once wrote a song called 'The Lights of Accrington' only to have it turned down by his music publisher. Whether true or false, it is a good story and concentrates the mind on what is or is not poetic.

Roger McGough, in his wonderful collection of poems *You at the Back*, shows how poetry can be inspired by the most unlikely of locations. There are poems about Birmingham and Cardiff, Huddersfield and Bradford. Not only do many towns and cities have an urban poetry, they evoke the resonance of the past. Who can travel through Yorkshire or South Wales without being reminded of images of winding gear against the setting sun? Who can travel to Liverpool or Newcastle without picturing the waterfront of yesteryear with its braying foghorns and towering cranes?

Our children should have a sense of pride in their locality and its history. Poetry about place can have a powerful impact on them.

Lesson 15

Lesson Plan

Objective: to write a poem about a locality.

Stimulus: Roger McGough's 'Bradford' (from *You at the Back, Selected Poems 1967-87*).

Sentence level: adjectives, proper nouns.

Shared writing: demonstrate how proper nouns can enrich a piece of descriptive writing.

Guided writing: describe a trip into town on a Saturday afternoon.

Bradford

Roger McGough

Saris billow in the wind like dhows off the shore
bus drivers whistle ragas above the traffic roar.
Late afternoon, and darkness already
elbowing its way through the crowded streets.
The pavements glister and are cold.
A lady, brittle with age, teeters along,
keeping balance with a shopping bag
in one hand and a giant box of cornflakes
in the other. Lovers arminarm home
to hot soup and a bath-for-two.
Everyone a passer-by or a passer-through.

Up at the university lectures are over for the day,
and students, ruddy
with learning, race back to the digs
to plan revolutions to end revolutions.

When asked why he had elected
to pursue mathematics in academic
seclusion, the old prof had answered:
'because there's safety in numbers.'

Teaching the lesson

Shared writing

After reading the poems, the teacher should instigate a discussion. How does Roger McGough achieve his effects? What role is played by:
- proper nouns
- speech
- imagery
- appeals to the senses
- humour
- cultural cross-references?

On the basis of this discussion, the teacher could demonstrate a poem, say 'Kirkby in the Rain', 'Morning Mist over Hartshead' or 'Snow on Moel Famau', drawing on the children's ideas.

Guided writing

The teacher could now discuss the scenario selected, a trip from Prescot to nearby Liverpool on the train. A provisional structure might go something like this:
- arriving at Lime Street station.
- the sights of Liverpool city centre, the weather.
- a notable incident, feelings at the end of the shopping trip.

(Teachers should amend their stimuli and content according to the locaility in which they teach.)

As ever, a strong last line is important. Could the writer coin an aphorism to sum up the day, for example, or is there simply a particularly resonant final image?

A visual aid might be a series of postcards, pictures of the city in question.

Examples of children's work

Liverpool

Steven Murray

Twelve noon
I got off the train
By that hideous clock
From Victorian times
On Lime Street station.

It was as cold as when you stick your hands
In the freezer
In Morrison's.

The Liver Birds were rocking to and fro.
The sky was as black
As the new Man U away kit.

The fat people were the pins
And the skinny people
were getting blown
like bowling balls.

The food was like leather
on two pieces of brown bread.

I asked could I have
A pair of Lacoste from Wade Smith Junior.
My mum said:
'What are they, a pair of socks?'
I thought,
I wish I was staying here
Rather than going back
To the one-eyed town.

Comments

Steven's poem has an identifiable and quirky sense of place. The use of brand names and place names adds significantly to the impact of the poem, as does the conversation between the poet and his mother. There are several striking images: the Liver Birds rocking; the food like leather; the people like skittles. The poem works successfully on a number of levels.

Extensions

One extension might be an elegiac invocation of the past. The teacher could collect images of their area's heritage and get the children to reflect on what is lost and what is unlamented. Some examples might be:
• the Liverpool or London docklands
• the coal mines of South Wales, Scotland, Yorkshire
• the fishing boats of Fleetwood, Hull or Aberdeen

Section 8: Narrative poems

Literature can be a contrary creature at times. The young reader and writer has finally got to grips with the distinction between a poem and a story, when along comes something called a narrative poem. Help! In order to come to terms with this form it is worth exploring both and drawing up some differences:

- How does the language differ?
- Is there a difference in the way the story and the poem appear on the page?
- Is there any difference in the imagery used?
- What about character, plotting, dialogue?
- Are different structures employed?

For the teacher, the question is this: is it better to tell the children the distinction or is it better to allow them to investigate for themselves and come up with some provisional judgements of their own?

In this section there are two different takes on the narrative poem.

Lesson 16

Lesson Plan

Objective: to write a short narrative poem, detailing a domestic incident.

Stimulus: excerpt from D.H. Lawrence's poem 'Man and a Bat' about a bat in his hotel room in Venice. (D.H Lawrence, *Selected Poems*).

Sentence level: exclamations.

Shared writing: demonstrate how to start the poem with an eye-catching event.

Guided writing: write a poem describing how a creature got into the house.

Man and Bat

D. H. Lawrence

When I went into my room, at mid-morning,
Say ten o'clock ...
My room, a crash-box over the great stone rattle
of the Via de' Bardi

When I went into my room at mid-morning
Why ... a bird!

A bird
Flying round the room in insane circles!
... A bat!

A disgusting bat
At mid-morning! ...

Out! Go out!

Round and round and round
With a twitchy, nervous, intolerable flight,
And a neurasthenic lunge,
And an impure frenzy;
A bat, as big as a swallow.

Out, out of my room!

So to drive him out, flicking with my white handkerchief: *Go!*
But he will not.

Round and round and round
In an impure haste,
Fumbling, a beast in air,
And stumbling, lunging and touching the walls, the bell-wires
About my room!

Teaching the lesson

Shared writing

After reading Lawrence's poem the class could discuss how a wild creature in a room can cause mayhem. Consider the perennial challenge of a wasp on a summer's day. How do people react? What do they use to trap the creature? What do they say? On the basis of the discussion the teacher could model a poem about, say, a sparrow trapped in the house, a common event some years ago before the decline of one of the best-loved British birds.

Guided writing

The teacher could now set a rough pattern for the poem:
• The creature appears.
• How did you, your mum, your dad react? What did they use to have a go at the creature?
• Did the creature go quietly? What happened next?
• How was it resolved?

The teacher could also suggest using brand names for the objects used. This creates more comic effect. Dialogue might also be considered. Exclamations might be used sparingly to spice up the action. Finally there is the old problem of the final line.

Mum and Wasp

Robert Ablewhite

When I was watching TV
This morning,
Eating my breakfast,
I heard a scream:

Ah!

A wasp.

Suddenly I turned my head
And my mum was having a go at it with the Mr Sheen.
That didn't work.
She then used the de-icer.
That didn't work.

The beast flew under the table.
Mum was on her hands and knees.
She shot under the table
With the cereal box.

Then there was a scream.
Help!
The wasp chased my mum up the stairs.

My dad came out of the bedroom.
He clutched his tie in his hands
And with one blow the wasp was dead.

My mum said:
'I could have done that.'

Comments

Robert's piece is lively and wonderfully humorous. He employs the things people say; the odd ways they react under pressure; gender roles, and a wry humour. His use of domestic objects such as the de-icer and the Mr Sheen are richly comic. When Mum at the end comments 'I could have done that' it concludes the wild action very satisfactorily. The whole poem has a breathless pace, reflecting the chase. One word lines such as *Ah!* or *Help!* contribute to this effect.

Extensions

There are many possible extensions:
- baby brother being sick, focusing on the race to find a bowl
- overflowing bath (water dripping through the ceiling, people's panicky reactions)
- telly on the blink (how people, particularly men, respond)

A marvellous stimulus for a school poem on this model is Allan Ahlberg's 'Dog in the playground'. In fact, just about any of Ahlberg's acutely observed school poems will inspire excitingly vivid writing.

Lesson 17

Lesson Plan

Objective: to write a narrative poem, detailing a historical event.

Stimulus: discussion of a battle between the Vikings and the Saxons.

Sentence level: the use of strong verbs and adjectives.

Shared writing: the structure of a narrative poem.

Guided writing: children write a poem on King Alfred's defeat of the Vikings.

Teaching the lesson

Shared writing

The key to this narrative poem is the symmetry of the two sides. A diagram might help showing the Saxon shield wall atop a hill and the Vikings massing at the foot of the slope. It is then a question of selecting repeated patterns to give the action a structure.

For the Saxons this is:

'On top of the hill
the Saxons stand …
And on their banner is a cross
On the final day of reckoning.'

For the Vikings it is:

'From the foot of the hill
the Vikings charge …
And on their banner is a raven
On the final day of reckoning.'

It is around this underlying structure that the events of the day can be described.

Guided writing

Once a satisfying structure has been established the pattern goes like this:
Verse 1: describe the Saxons at the top of the hill.
Verse 2: describe the Vikings' charge.
Verse 3: describe the coming together of the two armies.
Verse 4: resolve the action.

Pictures of the Saxons and Vikings, labelled with the names of the various weapons, might help. The teacher should stress that the more vivid the picture they paint the more successful the poem will be.

Examples of children's work

On the final day of reckoning

Adam Hilton, Year 5

On top of the hill
The Saxons stand.
They lock their shields
In a wall of iron.
Their armour flashes
 in the sun.
Their swords glisten
In the golden light.
And on their banner is a cross
On the final day of reckoning.

From the foot of the hill
The Vikings charge.
Their axes flash
In the glistening sun.
The Berserkers strip
From shoulder to waist.
They run and roar
Like wolves and demons.
And on their banner is a raven
On the final day of reckoning.

In the press of battle
Two armies meet.
They drive their swords
Into their enemies.
Blood stains the ground
And feet trample the dead
On the final day of reckoning.

But when the day is done
The Vikings break and run.
Crows feast on the dead
And shields litter the ground.
Only the cross flies now
On the final day of reckoning.

Comments

By using the repeated lines Adam creates a very convincing narrative of the battle. Rather than becoming a shapeless sequence of events, it is transformed into a well-structured, lyrical evocation of the titanic, deciding battle. Adam incorporates personal knowledge, the Berserkers, and vivid imagery: *They run and roar like wolves and demons*. He doesn't force rhymes. Rather, he chooses one telling couplet:

'But when the day is done
the Vikings break and run.'

The effect is extremely rich and eye-catching.

Extensions

By deconstructing a number of narrative poems, the teacher can show the children how to evoke a historical event.

You could try:
• Boudicca's final battle with the Romans
• a gladiatorial combat in the Colosseum
• the sinking of the *Mary Rose* or the *Titanic*
• the Battle of Britain
• the evacuation of Dunkirk
• the D-Day landings
• Martin Luther King's march over Selma Bridge
• Nelson Mandela's release from prison
• the Suffragettes' protests for votes for women
• The launch of Brunel's great ships

Section 9: Prayers

There are a number of different sub-genres of poetry which can deliver very striking results. The prayer is one such variety. In Paul Cookson's indispensable anthology *The Works* there is a useful section on prayers.

Good anthologies like this one are a godsend to the teacher of writing. They offer a way in to that repertoire of styles and genres to which I referred earlier. By deconstructing the techniques used by the poet, the teacher can then reconstruct them into a vital, well-organised piece of creative writing.

Lesson 18

Lesson Plan

Objective:	to write a poem in the form of a prayer.
Stimulus:	'Let No One Steal Your Dreams' by Paul Cookson.
Sentence level:	alternative patterns of sentences.
Shared writing:	establishing the format 'Let ...'
Guided writing:	write a prayer for an England victory in the World Cup.

Let No One Steal Your Dreams
Paul Cookson

Let no one steal your dreams
Let no one tear apart
The burning of ambition
That fires the drive inside your heart.

Let no one steal your dreams
Let no one tell you that you can't
Let no one hold you back
Let no one tell you that you won't.

Set your sights and keep them fixed
Set your sights on high
Let no one steal your dreams
Your only limit is the sky.

Let no one steal your dreams
Follow your heart
Follow your soul
For only when you follow them
Will you feel truly whole.

Set your sights and keep them fixed
Set your sights on high
Let no one steal your dreams
Your only limit is the sky.

Teaching the lesson

Shared writing

Prayers tend to have a distinctive pattern. In this lesson we are using one form:

> 'Let me not fall into misfortune.
> Let me see the error of my ways.'

After reading a number of poems and looking at the ways in which they are constructed, the teacher can, with the children, select the form for their poem. She could perhaps model a poem. She can then set the children to work to explore their own ideas.

Guided writing

Having established the format, the teacher can now ask the children to think what would get in the way of England winning the World Cup. These ideas, developing out of brainstorming, become the raw material of the poem. With a good ending, a successful poem can be written.

A prayer for an England Victory

Matthew Garrett, Year 5

Let Beckham's metatarsal heal.
Let Owen's hamstring not go ping.
Let us score in every match.
Let Heskey not fall over.
Let the three lions roar away
The super eagles.
Let them say: 'It's all over.'
It will be when we win.

Comments

Matthew's poem very effectively harnesses the prayer form to deliver its wry commentary on England's performance in the 2002 World Cup on the eve of defeat by Brazil. He follows the structure faithfully, adding his own humorous verdict.

Extensions

Prayers could be used for any aspirational writing:
- a prayer for a better world
- a prayer for a cleaner environment
- a prayer for a happier school
- a prayer for peace in the world
- a prayer for a fun family holiday

Section 10: Elegies

Elegies, like prayers, tend to follow a distinctive pattern. They reflect feelings of loss after the passing of a person, a place, a time. They work especially well after some event and can be used very successfully in Personal, Social and Health Education lessons.

Lesson 19

Lesson Plan

Objective: to write an elegy.

Stimulus: 'It's Not the Same Any More' by Paul Cookson.

Sentence level: use of repetition and questioning.

Shared writing: demonstrating the elegy form, and adding the use of questions to give a simple structure to the poem.

Guided writing: an elegy for George Harrison.

It's Not the Same Any More
Paul Cookson

It's not the same since Patch died.
Sticks are sticks.
Never thrown, never fetched.

It's not the same any more.
Tennis balls lie still and lifeless.
The urge to bounce them has gone.

It's not the same now.
I can't bring myself to whistle.
There's no reason to do so.

His collar stands on the hook
and his name tag and lead are dusty.

His basket and bowl are in a plastic bag
lying at an angle on a garage shelf.

My new slippers will never be chewed
and I've no excuse for my lack of homework any more.

I can now watch the football in peace, uninterrupted.
No frantic barking and leaping just when it gets to the goal.

I don't have to share my sweets and biscuits
and then wipe the dribbling drool off my trouser legs.

It's just not the same any more.
When Patch died a small part of me died too.
All that's left is a mound of earth
and my hand-made cross beneath the apple tree.

All that's left are the memories.
Thousands of them.

It's just not the same any more.

Teaching the lesson

Shared writing

After reading Paul Cookson's poem, and clarifying in discussion what an elegy is, the teacher can introduce the structure they will use – the use of questioning, asking where George and his achievements have gone. She can model the opening to show how the structure is established. This is the launchpad of the whole poem.

Guided writing

Once the format is established the teacher can concentrate on the transformation of ideas into lines of poetry through questions. When I taught this lesson George Harrison had just died. With the Year 4 class I discussed the Beatles' lyrics, especially those written by George Harrison, showed them pictures and LP covers and related anecdotes from my childhood in the Sixties as a fan of the Fab Four. Out of this immersion in the rhythms of the Mersey sound came a very affecting poem.

In Memoriam, George Harrison

Philippa Kelly

It's not the same since George died.
Songs are songs,
Always played, always sung.
It's not the same any more.
A little bit of Liverpool has died.
Where is it now?
Where is the guitar?
Where is the sitar?
Where is the quiet one?
Where are the loveable mop tops?
Where is 'When my guitar gently weeps'?
Where is 'Something'?
Where is 'Here comes the sun?'
Where is 'She loves you, yeah, yeah, yeah?'
Where is the one who stunned the world?
Where is the religious one?
Where is the Mersey sound in the background?
Where is all the fame?

Comments

Philippa's poem is a synthesis of two elements:
- a stimulus which drew the pupils' attention. This class was in Prescot, Merseyside.
- a simple but effective structure, essentially consisting, similar to the list poems, of the cumulative force of a series of questions.

Probably the main choice Philippa had to make was which line to close with. Selecting 'Where is all the fame?' creates a real emotional impact at the end of the poem.

An elegy works for any historical or religious figure. The Marvyn Gaye song, for example, 'Abraham, Martin and John' is elegiac in tone about Lincoln, Luther King and Kennedy. Elegies could also be written for times or communities. Here are some ideas:

• Martin Luther King
• the mining communities
• the *Titanic*
• the glory that was Rome
• Boudicca

Section 11: Altered images

People often dismiss flights of fancy as somehow trivial and lightweight. They are wrong. Stories and poems that invent worlds, or look at this one in a new and interesting way, are a way of commenting on the inconsistencies, absurdities and cruelties of our world.

Lesson 20

Lesson Plan

Objective:	to write a poem revealing an alternative view of the world.
Stimulus:	'Tonight at Noon' by Adrian Henri.
Sentence level:	sentence structure.
Shared writing:	demonstrate use of the line *In my upsy downsy world* or *Tonight at noon* to give structure.
Guided writing:	'In My Upsy Downsy World' or 'Tonight at Noon'.

Tonight at Noon
Adrian Henri

Tonight at noon
supermarkets will advertise 3p EXTRA on everything
Tonight at noon
Children from happy families will be sent to live in a home
Elephants will tell each other human jokes
America will declare peace on Russia
World War I generals will sell poppies in the streets on November 11th
The first daffodils of autumn will appear
When the leaves fall upwards to the trees

Tonight at noon
Pigeons will hunt cats through city bakyards
Hitler will tell us to fight on the beaches and on the landing fields
A tunnel full of water will be built under Liverpool
Pigs will be sighted flying in formation over Woolton
and Nelson will not only get his eye back but his arm as well
White Americans will demonstrate for equal rights

in front of the Black House
and the monster has just created Dr Frankenstein

Girls in bikinis are moonbathing
Folksongs are being sung by real folk
Artgalleries are closed to people over 21
Poets get their poems in the Top 20
Politicians are elected to insane asylums
There's jobs for everyone and nobody wants them
In back alleys everywhere teenage lovers are kissing in broad daylight
In forgotten graveyards everywhere the dead will quietly bury the living
and
You will tell me you love me
Tonight at noon.

Teaching the lesson

Shared writing

To start the lesson the teacher could read 'Tonight at Noon'. She should concentrate on taking archetypal images and reversing them:
• fire fighters starting fires
• cats chasing dogs
• leaves rising up to the trees
• babies changing their parents' nappies.

It may help to sort these alternative images of the world into categories:
• the natural world
• physical processes
• jobs
• historical figures and famous people.

The teacher can then demonstrate one category on the board linking them from time to time with the repeated line *Tonight at noon* or *In my upsy downsy world*.

Guided writing

The main challenge of the poem once the children have the format clear in their mind is to move the lines about. What works best is to put similar lines into pairs or small groups e.g:

> 'Isaac Newton fell on the apple,
> Bethany invented calculus.'

A good strategy is to go away in groups or as individuals, depending on the children's preference, and brainstorm ideas. They can then cut these up and rearrange them until they get the best fit. The effect of the poem relies on the originality of the alternative images of the world.

Adrian Henri's poem ends:

> 'And you will tell me you love me.'
> Tonight at noon.'

This will obviously not fit with younger children. It is worth discussing other endings. They may choose something like:

> 'And children tidy their rooms
> tonight at noon.'

Or perhaps:

> 'And armies declare peace on Earth
> in an upsy downsy world.'

Examples of children's work

The Upsy Downsy World

Calum Robson, Year 3

In an upsy downsy world humans are endangered
And live in zoos.
Animals rule the world.
People write upside down.
In my upsy downsy world
People put full stops at the start of the sentence
And put capital letters at the enD.
In my upsy downsy world
Rabbits eat tigers.
In my upsy downsy world
When people jump
They go underground,
People dig holes in the sky,
People walk on their hands,
People are born old and die young.
Humans lived 65,000,000 years ago

And dinosaurs live now.
Animals buy pet humans,
Prey catches predators,
Isaac Newton fell on the apple,
Bethany invented calculus,
Dogs walk people,
People write backward,
Silly people are sensible
In an upsy downsy world.

Tonight at Noon

Chloe Dixon, Year 7

Tonight at noon
Scallies will wipe graffiti off walls,
And car drivers will get a fine
For driving too slow.
Tonight at noon
Babies will give birth to mums,
Children will teach teachers.
Tonight at noon
Pigs will fly,
Michael Owen will be rubbish
At football
And clocks will ask us the time.
Tonight at noon vegetarians
Will eat meat
And elephants will chase mice.
Finally,
Tonight at noon,
Day will turn into night.

Tonight at Noon

Nathan Fisher, Year 8

Tonight at noon
England will lift the NatWest trophy.
Tonight at noon
Mike Tyson will lose an ear
In a fight,
Dogs will take humans for a walk,
Rivaldo will skip over
A two-footed challenge,
Bin Laden will pick up
A Nobel Peace Prize
As he walks up the aisle
With George Bush
And all guns will be destroyed
Tonight at noon.

Comments

As with the list poems, in the hands of these young writers a relatively simple structure can prove an effective vehicle for quite startling ideas. Calum shows a precocious intelligence for a seven year old to come up with lines about Isaac Newton or calculus while both Chloe and Nathan take advantage of the format to launch some social and political commentary. Creative writing provides young people with a rare opening in an often over-prescriptive curriculum to explore their own views of the world.

Extensions

As a variation on the theme children could explore:
• In a world without wars
• If I ruled the world
• If I won the National Lottery
• An alien's account of a trip to Earth.

It is all about giving the children the opportunity to write about their ideas about the world they live in in an imaginative way.

Section 12: Cross curricular links

Writing need not take place only in English lessons. There are opportunities for creative writing in personal and social education, R.E., geography and history. In modern education there has sometimes been a tendency among a minority of teachers to 'play safe' and over-use worksheets. In reality there is nothing safe about this practice of 'death by a thousand worksheets'. It is dull fare for the young mind and fails children. Writing becomes truncated and dependent upon the teacher. Instead of the teacher modelling the tools of good writing, the teacher offers a format which enshrines low expectations.

The poems in this section are taken from a cross-curricular project carried out at Prescot County Primary School on Merseyside. In a booklet produced for the school library and parents the poems were accompanied by photographs, excerpts from the school log book between 1939 and 1945, historical research, interviews and letters. The finished product is a celebration of the children's work, a tribute to a generation that gave so much, and a resource for other pupils. I would argue that this kind of extended study contributes more to children's development than a curriculum of individual, unrelated lessons trapped within the confines of subject boundaries.

Lesson 21

Lesson Plan

Objective: to write a poem using a repeated pattern.

Stimulus: list poems and a discussion of the day war broke out.

Sentence level: questions.

Shared writing: modelling sentences in the form of questions.

Guided writing: write a poem: 'Where were you?'

Teaching the lesson

Shared writing

The teacher should base the lesson on research into the day war broke out. In the Prescot project the children listened to the memories of an 80-year-old who remembered the day vividly. Her recollections became the raw material of the poem. The teacher then demonstrated how to put across the ideas. Each sentence was a question and included two ideas rather than one, e.g:

'Were you out shopping or home by your wireless?'

The line: 'Where were you when the war broke out?' started and ended the poem, giving it a clear structure.

Guided writing

Once the pattern of the poem is established, it becomes a question of moving the lines about for maximum effect.

Examples of children's work

Where Were You?

Victoria Kearly, Year 3

Where were you when the war broke out?
Where were you when it started?
Were you in school or on a tram?
Were you at the corner shop or on the ferry?
Were you in the garden or the living room?
Where were you when the war broke out?

Where Were You?

Tom Broadfoot, Year 3

Where were you when the war broke out?
Where were you when it started?
Were you at the docks or sitting in school?
Were you in the corner shop or up in your room?
Were you at the park or at Lime Street station?
Where were you when the war broke out?

Lesson 22

Lesson Plan

Objective: to write a poem imagining a historical event.

Stimulus: interview with an older person from the community who was a child during the war. Alternatively, an account taken from video or TV.

Shared writing: demonstrate the pattern of the poem using the lines: 'I've got a Donald Duck gas mask' and, in the middle of the poem, 'And oh! How I hate it' to structure it.

Guided writing: children write their own poems: 'I've got a Donald Duck gas mask'.

Teaching the lesson

Shared writing

Drawn from the interview, the teacher uses the structural lines as a framework around which to explore the children's ideas of what it must have been like inside a gas mask. The simple structure allows the children to turn a few simple sentence of description into an effective poem.

Guided writing

Once the structure is established the children are free to communicate their ideas, closing with the repeated line.

Examples of children's work

I've got a Donald Duck Gas Mask

Christopher Kay, Year 3

I've got a Donald Duck gas mask
And I keep it in a box.
I put it on so I can breathe
And oh! How I hate it.
It smells all rubbery
When I'm inside.
This is how I feel:

It's hot inside the gas mask.
I feel itchy and roasting.
I've got a Donald Duck gas mask.

Comments

Christopher's poem exploits the structure to communicate how it might feel to wear a gas mask. Needless to say, the children all got to try on a gas mask during the project. By replicating the way the grandparent talked about her childhood, Christopher has written convincingly in the voice of a wartime child.

Extensions

There are few experiences poetry could not communicate. It really helps to hear somebody reminisce, to listen to a recorded interview or to read a historical account. This enables the children to reproduce the spoken word in poetry. It combines speaking and listening, in addition to writing skills. Teachers could try:
- a modern-day re-drafting of Martin Luther King's 'I have a dream' speech
- a poem about unemployment in the Thirties
- a poem about being a soldier on Hadrian's Wall. The children could read the letters discovered on the wall and W.H Auden's wonderful 'Roman Wall Blues' (p. 6).

Here is one final poem from the Prescot Project. It is a fairly simple piece of wordplay which uses a simple structure, but it shows the kind of work which can be produced by this approach.

No joke

Stephen Burns

Imagine it's happened.
Imagine they're here.
The German army has made it.
It's Liverpool next.
There'll be guns in Gateacre
Or soldiers in Speke,
Aeroplanes in Allerton
Or planes in Prescot,
The dead in Dingle
Or bombs in Bootle.
You never know,
Maybe even Nazis in Netherton.

Lesson 23

Lesson Plan

Objective: to turn a recollection into a poem.

Stimulus: interview with a grandparent about rationing.

Sentence level: writing lists. Use of colon.

Shared writing: writing a list correctly.

Guided writing: using the list form to write a poem: 'Last night I dreamed of bananas'.

Teaching the lesson

Shared writing

Having listened to the interview with a grandparent who was a child during the war, the children put themselves in the place of a youngster during rationing.

Demonstrate how to construct a list and discuss the kind of opening and closing lines the pupils might use gives a template for the poem.

Guided writing

Missing favourite foods is a subject close to the hearts of most children. The teacher discusses with the children where they would be most likely to dream of food. This gives the lines that pattern the poem. From then on the only guidance necessary is looking at putting more than one item on each line to get a rhythm.

Examples of children's work

Last Night I Dreamed of Bananas

Aimi Tipton

Last night as I lay awake in bed
I dreamed of bananas
But that's not all.
I dreamed of:
Chocolate and coconut,
Cheese and tea,

Eggs and meat.
How I hope that dream comes true.

Comments

Aimi's use of a simple list, combined with a strong structure delivers an excellent little vignette of a poem that evokes the privations of the war years.

Extensions

Lists can be incorporated in many historical or geographical poems. You could try a version of this:

Everest

Here you stand
At the top of the world.
Below you,
You will see:
Glaciers gleaming in the sunlight,
Crags and boulders,
Rock faces
As sheer as any
In the worlds of ancient myths.
Here you stand
At the top of the world.
Will you ever see another thing
To match it?

Many historical or geographical experiences could be accessed using this simple device.

Lesson 24

Lesson Plan

Objective: to write a poem using a repeated pattern.

Stimulus: interview with a grandparent. (When asked: 'What do you think about the war now?' he replied simply: 'Never again.')

Sentence level: different sentence structures.

Shared writing: use of the rhetorical device: Never again.

Guided writing: children write a poem 'Never Again!'

Teaching the lesson

Shared writing

After listening to the interview, the teacher focuses on how to use the rhetorical device, repeating the phrase *Never again* at the start of each line. In addition, it is necessary to discuss opening and closing lines to add structure and depth.

Guided writing

Using the basic structure, the teacher now uses the technique, seen above, of putting two items on each line to create a rhythm. The final item of the list, perhaps the most striking, might be the only one to stand alone, giving it extra force.

Examples of children's work

Never Again!

Rory Kerr, Year 5

It was fifty years ago,
The end of a terrible war.
Millions say:
Never again!
Never again the destruction and the deaths.
Never again the darkness and the sadness.

Never again the noises and the bombs.
Never again the fighting and the killing.
Never again the horror of war.
That's why we say:
Never again!

Comments

Rory utilises the structure of the poem to create a very striking example of rhetoric. The *Never again* lines are not strictly sentences. They do not, of course, have a verb. But grammar is a tool to communicate meaning. It can sometimes be subverted to achieve effect. The poem is spare and very powerful.

Extensions

The music from the film *Gladiator* might provide an effective stimulus for a poem about the Colosseum in ancient Rome.

When we are free

When we are free
We will never raise our hands
Against our brothers.
When we are free
We will use our strength
Only to plough the earth.
When we are free
We will be men
By the beat of our blood
And the dreams in our minds
And no longer
By our muscles alone.
When we are free
Our blood will only be spilt
In defence of our homes, our families,
Our love of life.
When we are free.

Section 13: Using music

Poetry has been called song without music. This is a pretty good stab at a definition though it ignores the musicality of rhythm. The links between music, song and poetry should be self-evident. Using music as a stimulus for poetry seems an obvious strategy. Just think how music contributes to film. There is an astonishing resonance in a musical score. Let's consider one well-known scene. Play the opening bars of 'Wonderful World' by Sam Cooke and ask three simple questions:

- Who was the guy?
- Who was the girl?
- Where was the car parked?

The answers are respectively:

- The guy was Harrison Ford
- The girl was Kelly McGillis
- The car was parked in a barn in Amish country.

The film is *Witness* and Sam Cooke's glorious song leads into one of the most finely-timed, well-studied love scenes in recent cinema. If thirty- or forty-something teachers can go misty-eyed at such moments, shouldn't we give children the opportunity to explore the links between music and poetry?

Teachers can use music extremely successfully to harness this kind of resonance.

Lesson 25

Lesson Plan

Objective: to write an anthem based on a piece of popular music.

Stimulus: 'Change is Gonna Come' by Sam Cooke (from *Portrait of a legend*, 1951-1964, ABKCO Music and Records).

Sentence level: contraction of *I have* to *I've*.

Shared writing: using the Sam Cooke song as a template to write an anthem.

Guided writing: writing a poem 'Changes' to reflect on good and bad features of the modern world.

Teaching the lesson

Shared writing

To lay the basis of the poem, the teacher can model an opening based on Sam Cooke's lyrics, then show how sentences starting *'I've seen ...'* form the main section of the poem, reflecting on the bad things the children have witnessed on TV or in their local community. Brain-storming ideas and modelling how the sentences can be written will inform the children's writing.

Guided writing

The chorus from the song forms the structure of the poem. Once the structure is established, the teacher can set the children to work, turning their own ideas into a coherent poem. The first section is modelled around a sentence structure:

'I've seen ...'

The second section is modelled around aspirations for the future:

'I want to see ...'

Finally, the children will draw on Sam Cooke's chorus to conclude the poem.

Changes

Abbie Molloy, Year 4

I was born by a river
In a little house,
And, like the river,
I keep on running.
I've seen walls full of graffiti.
I've seen cars getting bombed.
I've seen a child, toys all snapped.
I've seen people with no home.
I've seen people who smoke and take drugs.
I've seen children getting kidnapped.
Change is gonna come.

I was born by a river
In a little house,
And , like the river,
I keep on running.
I want to see peace spreading across the world.
I want to see the air clean,
Not polluted.
I want to see bombs thrown away like rubbish.
I want to see no more wars.
Change has got to come.
Oh yes it will.

Comments

Even very young writers, given a clear structure to work with, and encouraged to use that structure to develop their own ideas, can come up with striking pieces of work. Abbie's poem shows how, at just eight, she has a formed strong views about the world around her. She expresses herself with clarity and achieves an emotional impact with some of her lines. See, for example, this line:

'I've seen a child, toys all snapped.'

Extensions

There are numerous pieces of music which can inspire good quality writing. Try these:

- Vivaldi's *Four Seasons* as a stimulus for descriptive poetry
- Holst's *The Planets* suite
- Dvorak's *New World* symphony describing perhaps a ship gliding into New York through the morning mist
- 'Imagine' by John Lennon
- 'Affirmation' by Savage Garden
- 'The Streets of Philadelphia' by Bruce Springsteen as a stimulus for a poem about homelessness
- 'She's Leaving Home' by the Beatles about children's relationships with their parents
- 'Eleanor Rigby' about loneliness
- 'Who's Gonna Take You Home?' by the Cars

Lesson 26

Lesson Plan

    Objective: to write a poem about place based on a song.

    Stimulus: 'Heart as Big as Liverpool' by Wah (from *The Handy Wah! Whole,* Sanctuary Records, 2000).

Sentence level: complex sentences.

Shared writing: a complex sentence structure.

Guided writing: Poem 'Heart as Big as ...'.

Teaching the lesson

Shared writing

Pete Wylie's song 'Heart as big as Liverpool' starts with the lines:

> 'When all the lights go out forever
> Somewhere on the edge of time.'

The teacher can adapt this to create a repeated structure the children can use. For example, it could go like this:

> 'When you've seen the sun go down
> over the Mersey,
> and you've seen the ferry
> ploughing to and fro.
> When you've seen the seagulls
> bickering over the water,
> and you've seen the buildings' reflections
> trembling in the waves,
> then you've got a heart
> as big as Liverpool.'

The structure therefore goes like this:

> 'When you've seen ...
> and you've seen ...
> then you've got a heart as big
> as Liverpool.'

This forms the basis of verses about what you see, what you hear, what you feel.

This needs teaching. Modelling this sentence shows, in context, how clauses work to build a sentence. In order to simplify and pace the poem, the teacher could make the first section or verse what the child sees, the second what he hears, and finally the third how he feels returning home.

Guided writing

Given the clear structure, the young writer can put their own ideas in place. The teacher needs to stress that this should be as visual, auditory, sensory and emotive as possible. They are writing an anthem to their home region. Proper nouns help achieve the effect.

Examples of children's work

Heart as Big as Merseyside

John Owens, Year 5

When you've seen
St George Hall
Standing stiff and still
And you've seen
Tidal waves of red
Flowing into Anfield,
And you've seen the Liver Birds
Looking out across the city,
You've got a heart as big as Merseyside.

When you've heard the roar of Anfield
And when you've heard
The seagulls crying,
And when you've heard
The famous sounds of the Beatles,
You've got a heart as big as Merseyside.

When you feel
The joy of being home
You really have got a heart as big as Merseyside.

Anthem: Heart as Big as Merseyside

Rebecca Jones, Year 5

When you've seen
The ferry gliding across the Mersey,
And you've seen Pleasure Land
With the cyclone blowing people off their feet,
And you've seen the Bluecoat School
With pupils in their royal blue blazers,
You've got a heart as big as Merseyside.
When you've heard the actors acting in the Empire Theatre,
And you've heard the crashing waves on New Brighton beach,
And you've heard the cathedral bells ringing
You've got a heart as big as Merseyside.
When you feel the joy of belonging
You really have got
A heart as big as Merseyside.

Heart as Big as Merseyside

Joe, Year 4

When you've seen
The water reflecting the sunset coming up,
And you've seen
The sun has finally risen,
You've got a heart as big as Merseyside.

When you've heard
The waves lapping onto the sand,
And you've heard
The crabs clicking their feet in the long, sharpy sand,
You've got a heart as big as Merseyside.

When you feel
The crabs' claws with razors
Slicing through your fingers,
And you feel
The rocks crumbling in your hand
Then you've got a heart as big as Merseyside.

When you feel
The joy of belonging
You really have a heart
As big as Merseyside.

Comments

All three children use the structure to reflect their own individual responses. A major influence in John's poem is his support for Liverpool Football Club. Rebecca's is full of the places she has been with her parents and the school she would clearly like to attend. Joe's is constructed around the fishing for crabs that takes place in places like New Brighton. Joe even invents his own adjective in the line: 'the long, sharpy sand.' Should this be corrected ? I would argue against. The meaning is clear and its inclusion resonates with the musicality of the city.

Extensions

Many localities have their own celebrations in music. Children in Newcastle could write their own versions of 'Fog on the Tyne', for example. In the absence of an obvious song around which to weave the children's observations, young writers anywhere could write a version of Bruce Springsteen's 'My Home Town' and explore what it means to them.

Chapter 4

Some additional ideas

Here are a few extra ideas which can produce good work from young people.

Epitaphs

An epitaph is an inscription on a tombstone. It tells you something about the person who is buried there. It can be in poetry or prose.

Epitaph 1

Here beneath this clay
I lie, one Marcus Jones.
No more will I see the light of day
All that's left of me is bones.

Epitaph 2

Here lies Polly Cell.
She came to a sticky end.
RIP

Epitaph 3

Here lies Humpty Dumpty.
People say he was cracked
But that might be a bad yolk.

Epitaph 4

U.N. Dead
Here he lies deep in the ground.
A word of warning –
Don't hang around!
Rest in Peace
(maybe).

Epitaphs work well in history, RE and PSHE lessons and are a very useful extension activity. Presented on gravestones, they make excellent display items.

Colour that emotion

Choose a human emotion such as jealousy, fear, anxiety, love, hate, anger, etc. Write a poem according to this formula:

- what colour is the emotion?
- what does it taste like?
- what does it smell like?
- what does it look like?
- what does it sound like?
- what does it feel like?

Hope

Hope is white, almost colourless.
It tastes like a snowflake on your tongue
And smells like a raindrop on a rose petal.
Hope looks like the space where love has just been standing.
It sounds like the shudder of your own breathing.
Hope teases.

These poems work well in PSHE and can make an excellent contribution to assemblies.

Food poems

Write poems with an adjective on each line (How it tastes? How it feels to touch? What it is like to bite?), then a sentence which sums up how it feels in your mouth. Write the poem on a piece of paper shaped like the food itself.

Lemon

Dimpled,
Waxy,
Soft,
Tangy,
It makes me wince.

Bacon

Reddish,
Crispy,
Crunchy,
Salty,
It teases my taste buds.

These poems make a good addition to science lessons on food.

Call and response

These poems ask questions then answer them.

Call and Response

Why does the sun rise?
– to drive away the night.
How does it begin the day?
– by washing its face in the dew.
Where does the darkness go?
– into empty hearts.
Why do people cry?
– to wash away the pain.
Why do they laugh?
– because pain doesn't last forever.
What does the future hold?
– Me in its hands.

Again, these poems work very well in PSHE.

Appendix

Bringing an author into school

Much of this book has been devoted to the notion of the teacher providing a model of the writing process, demonstrating to their students how to use language which is clear, expressive, imaginative, and even musical to communicate their ideas. There is, of course, another human resource which can be tapped and that is the writer.

Working with people who write for a living is a valuable experience. It demystifies writing and shows that it is something anyone can do. It demonstrates that expressing yourself through the medium of the written word can be both fun and emotionally rewarding. It helps introduce young people to the diversity and richness of contemporary British writing.

Writing Together is an initiative jointly organised by the Department for Education and Skills, QCA, Booktrust, Arts Council England and the Poetry Society. It is worth quoting at length from its publication *Bringing Writers into Schools*:

'Why a writer?

Inviting a writer into school:
- is inspiring and exciting for pupils and teachers
- encourages pupils to write and to see writing as worthwhile
- supports the teaching of both writing and reading
- pays dividends in pupils' development right across the curriculum, particularly in terms of planning, drafting and revising work
- encourages awareness of styles, imagery, structure and audience
- promotes the sharing of ideas and approaches
- helps young people to learn how inspiration is derived from a very wide range of sources
- provides a fresh awareness of the process and purpose of creative writing
- gives pupils the opportunity to think about how a book is created and where it all begins and ends
- promotes the idea of writing as a profession and writers as real people.'

Secretary of State for Education Charles Clarke says in the same booklet:
'Writing Together promotes creativity and raises standards because it brings together teachers, pupils and writers in a unique partnership. I am convinced of the value of writers in schools and look forward to these conferences developing effective approaches to writer visits and residencies so that they become a permanent part of the Key Stage 3 curriculum.'

For so many teachers who have often felt frustrated because of the pressures of a very prescriptive curriculum and testing regime, this can only come as a welcome statement. The only addendum I would make would be the Key Stage 1, 2 and 4 curriculums too.

Have clear objectives
It is important to have clear objectives. Do you want a long term or short term residence? What kind of writer do you want: a poet, a novelist, a non-fiction writer? With what age range will they be expected to work? Do you want them to give an author talk with questions and answers or would you like somebody who can lead writing workshops? Would the children benefit most from a mixture of the two? Will you incorporate sales of the author's books into the day? It should be self-evident that book ownership plays an extremely important part in encouraging young readers.

There are other considerations. What will be the outcome of the residence or visit? Will work be displayed around the school? Will it be published in an anthology or on the Internet? What follow-up will there be? Are parents or members of the local community going to be involved? Could you organise a celebration of achievement?

Find a suitable writer
Expect to pay a minimum fee of £250 a day, plus travel expenses and accommodation if required. Remember that writers have to earn a living too. For every J. K. Rowling, Jacqueline Wilson or Terry Pratchett there are hundreds of struggling writers. The Society of Authors estimates that 75% of authors receive an income comparable to a cleaner! This is a modest investment. Many schools invite several writers a year and their students gain a great deal from the experience. Information on funding can be found on the website of the National Literacy Trust: www.literacytrust.org.uk

Many authors have their own websites and you will be able to find out if they do school visits. You can also find writers who have experience of working in schools by contacting Booktrust, the Poetry Society, the National Association of Writers in Education or the various regional databases (information below). Your local library may also arrange visits by authors. Building a relationship with the library should be central to the ethos of the school anyway. The Artscape directory ensures that all individuals listed have enhanced disclosure checks from the Criminal Records Bureau and appropriate insurance.

Allow plenty of time between the initial contact and the visit. Many writers, especially those who have appeared on the shortlists of the many book awards, tend to be booked six to eight months ahead. I have lost count of the number of schools who have called me in February to ask if I can come on World Book Day in March. I usually answer: 'Which March?'

Practical advice

Agree the total cost, including travel and accommodation, well in advance. Check whether the author is VAT registered. If possible, arrange for the cheque to be ready on the day. If this is impractical, give the writer a rough idea when they can expect payment. The penniless writer waiting for a cheque to come in the post isn't completely fiction.

Have a clear line of communication: a phone number or email address. Arrange for the author to be picked up if they are coming by public transport. If they are driving, make sure they have a map and clear directions well in advance.

Negotiate the timetable of events with the writer. Don't spring a list of demands on them on arrival. This will only cause tension. Discuss the room in which they will work and check what equipment they will need. Do your best to avoid interruptions. Dragging children out of an engrossing session to see the dentist or attend an assembly is hugely frustrating and counter-productive.

Make arrangements for breaks and for lunch. The author should be provided with a bottle of spring water during sessions. Coffee and biscuits during breaks always go down well. Lunch should be provided. Check dietary requirements in advance. Don't expect the writer to fend for him or herself. Remember, they are in unfamiliar surroundings. We all need a little TLC. I heard of one famous poet who asked for a school lunch. He was told no and had to eat fish and chips on the sea front!

Prepare the children in advance. They should be familiar with at least one of the writer's titles. It helps to have looked up the author's website. Do your homework. I was once introduced to 200 Year 8s as follows:

'This is...what was your name again? ... Right, this is Mr Gibson ... What ... Oh, Gibbons! I'm afraid I haven't read any of your books, but teachers are busy people. Well, this is Year 8. Off you go.'

Make sure the writer is supported at all times. Don't leave them alone with 32 children. Don't do your marking at the back. Get involved. Working with a writer acts as INSET. What's more, it is enjoyable and enriching.

Contact the local media to publicise the visit. It is good for the school, good for the writer and good for the pupils.

Bibliography

This is the absolutely bare minimum English teacher's toolbox of the best in traditional and modern poetry. Every school should have a teachers' resource shelf including these volumes. This selection will provide you with all the models and stimuli you will ever need and, incidentally, enormously enrich your life.

The Works, ed. Paul Cookson (Macmillan)

The Works 2, ed. Brian Moses and Pie Corbett (Macmillan)

Read Me 1, (Macmillan)

Read Me 2, (Macmillan)

The Rattle Bag, ed. Seamus Heaney and Ted Hughes (Faber)

Collected Poems for Children, Gareth Owen (Macmillan)

Please Mrs Butler, Allan Ahlberg (Puffin)

Heard it in the Playground, Allan Ahlberg (Puffin)

The Mersey Sound, Adrian Henri, Roger McGough, Brian Patten (Penguin)

You at the Back, Roger McGough (Penguin)

It Takes One to Know One, Gervaise Phinn (Puffin)

My Gang, ed. Brian Moses (Macmillan)

Did I Hear You Write? Michael Rosen (Five Leaves Publications)

Carrying the Elephant, Michael Rosen (Penguin)

The Very Best of Paul Cookson (Macmillan)

The Puffin Book of Twentieth Century Children's Verse, ed. Brian Patten (Puffin)

The Nation's Favourite Children's Poems (BBC)

To Rhyme or Not to Rhyme? Sandy Brownjohn (Hodder and Stoughton)

Books for Keeps (children's book magazine), 6, Brightfield Road, Lee, London SE12 8QF.

Carousel (children's book magazine), The Saturn Centre, 54-76, Bissell Street, Birmingham B5 7HX.

To contact me, Alan Gibbons, about anything in this volume email me via my website:

www.alangibbons.com

A final note

Readers will have noticed a definite bias in this book. The city of Liverpool casts a long shadow over its pages. The thing is, I taught here for twenty years so, though there are also pieces of work from all over the UK, a certain Merseyside dominance is unavoidable. Sorry!